PROFESSIONAL SMITHING

TRADITIONAL TECHNIQUES
FOR
DECORATIVE IRONWORK,
WHITESMITHING, HARDWARE,
TOOLMAKING, AND LOCKSMITHING

DONALD STREETER

With photographs and drawings
by the author

ASTRAGAL PRESS
Lakeville, Minnesota

Book design by Elaine Golt Gongora.

Library of Congress Catalog Card Number: 95-76818
ISBN 10: 1-879335-66-2
ISBN 13: 978-1-879335-66-0

Published by
The Astragal Press
An Imprint of Finney Company
8075 215th Street West
Lakeville, Minnesota 55044

www.finneyco.com
www.astragalpress.com

Printed in the United States of America

For my daughters,
Sandra and Nancy

ACKNOWLEDGMENTS

The one person to whom I owe the most is my brother, Guy Streeter, who worked with me for many years, building both the shop and the trade. Together we learned and taught each other.

My acknowledgment goes to James C. Sorber, from whose collection of American wrought iron, the English pipe tongs, swivel toaster, and standing broiler were adapted or reproduced.

Particularly, I appreciate the interest shown by Peter Ross, whose kind intercession brought publisher and author together.

CONTENTS

PREFACE

Every labor-saving invention eliminates a hand skill. The Industrial Revolution eventually caught up with the smiths, as it did with all other hand craftsmen. They and their skills passed into history, unmissed as the technological world burst upon us. The loss is that trade secrecy kept others from sharing their knowledge.

Now, in a new generation, old skills are being rediscovered and forgotten tools used again, in new and exciting ways. In 1976 Southern Illinois University at Carbondale mounted a landmark exhibition, Iron Solid Wrought USA, the first within memory to celebrate iron forging as an artist's medium. A few years ago not one art school offered a course in this field; now several do so.

The Artist-Blacksmiths Association of North America (ABANA) unites smiths, young and old, with a mutual exchange of information about ironwork. Foundations provide grants for craft programs of all kinds, and a buying public exists that appreciates the individuality and beauty of good hand workmanship. This renaissance is good news. Now it is possible to see a practicing smith at work without going to a museum village.

If it is important to preserve the products of past crafts, it is equally important to preserve the crafts themselves. Culture includes not merely the collection and admiration of artifacts, but also their making. In this sense, culture is more meaningful as a verb than as a noun. For to culture means to nourish, cherish, encourage, improve. This means life, not death.

As long as masters have been creating art, others have been studying the masters' creations, seeking to divine their secrets. Copying is not done for the copy alone, but also for mastery of the skill that made the original. A smith who learns the method by which the master worked increases his own skills, and probably finds an easier way to work. After all, the masters whose work has come down to us were themselves the beneficiaries of a thousand years of previous practice.

What follows in these pages is not a course of lessons, but a case book of some of the work that has passed through my shop. It records only the way one smith works.

I welcome all new smiths to this fascinating craft, and admire the variety and creativity of the work being done at today's forges.

1 INTRODUCTION

In order to help the reader follow some of the techniques shown in the following pages, a description of the shop and its layout is the best way to begin. The main work area is eighteen by thirty feet, with an eight-foot ceiling, affording room to raise a sledge. An attic provides storage space for seldom-used materials. The forge lies at one end, with a fire-safe floor of brick laid in sand, eleven by twenty feet. The single chimney is flanked by two forges, back to back, with a tool supply for each.

The Main Forge Area
The need for speedy decisions leaves little room for disorganization. Tools required should be within reach, and those not needed should be out of the way. Enough clutter will develop with the best of intentions; tools that are used only occasionally are stored elsewhere. Because most of the work done here is small in size, no great space is required, so it is possible to move from forge to anvil or vise in a couple of steps. The anvil is so placed that when working the fire, one makes only a quarter turn to face the anvil. This seems to be a more practical arrangement than having to make a complete about-face from one to the other, when more time is lost in making the move. This way, a turn of the head shows whether the anvil is clear and ready for work.

In the photo on page 3, along the wall at the left is an iron rack of plank shelves, open at each end, in which iron bar stock, cut in four- to five-foot lengths, is kept. Longer bars are seldom needed. They are stored in another rack, and are cut and fed to this one as the work may require. It is unsafe to stack bar stock on the floor.

The forge is built of brick, three feet high by about three feet square, high enough for a tall smith and light work, and large enough for most work of this shop. On the near side of the forge lies an old cast-iron flat sash weight which serves as a welding block. It is bedded in fine coal and is used when welding thin material, to save time in moving from fire to weld. On it is the flux box and a wire brush for scale removal. A forge rake and straight poker lie behind the block. At the smith's end of the forge is a bar of two-inch-square steel set on end and held in place with staples; this is used as an anvil when pointing quantities of nails. In the right foreground stands a bickern, which is portable and is set into a gum stump. Behind it is one of the shop's tongs racks.

An adjustable iron helper, for supporting ends of bars, appears in the left foreground. Above it is the hammer rack with a group of cross- and ball-peens, and a five-pound, short-handled, double-faced sledge. Above the rack, in rows, are anvil tools such as hardies, swages, bicks, punches, and mandrels. Above them are spring clamps for holding round stock in the vise when upsetting for rivet heads and the like.

The leg vise, with six-inch jaws, is hung on a railroad tie set two feet into the ground. Beyond it, under a window hidden by the iron rack, is a bench on which is thick cast-iron plate, twenty by forty inches. It is the type bed from an old cylinder printing press, and makes a fine surface plate for flattening strap hinges. It is calibrated along two edges, and its surface is scribed with intersecting lines that form three angles of 120°, for spacing and aligning tripod legs for candlestands and similar work. Storage space for jigs and such is under the bench. On the wall above the bench hang spring dies for forming knobs and collars under the power hammer, and on the plate is a rod cutter.

On the floor is the slack tub and fire sprinkler, and a cast-iron cone mandrel for forming rings

Main forge area, Donald Streeter's shop, Franklinville, N.J.

The anvil.

and bands. Under the far window is another anvil and tool rack. On the wall to the left of the window are staple benders and hinge-eye benders.

The Anvil

The anvil, one of three alike in the shop, is a Kohlswa Swedish steel blacksmiths' pattern weighing one hundred and fifty pounds. It rests on a cherry stump set two feet into the earth, with a hardy held by a staple in the wood. It is not strapped down, because the various anvils have been altered to suit different uses, and are changed from time to time to suit the work. Since they are squarely bedded, and the work is comparatively light, such greater stability as strapping would furnish is not crucial. One anvil has been calibrated at its top front edge in inches and half inches, to be read from above, so measures can be taken without reaching for a rule, with consequent heat loss. The welding block is also calibrated along one edge, to aid in checking

Secondary forge area.

lengths of small strap hinges. The hammer is a three-pound cross-peen.

The Secondary Forge Area

This embraces the second forge and its family of tools, which is similar to the other. At this forge, however, the vise is set so as to be free-standing, in order that longer bars can be bent without obstruction. Also at this side of the shop is the acetylene welding equipment, not used much in production but valuable for welding and brazing jigs and silver-soldering brass doorknobs. On the wall beyond the anvil are ranks of headers for nails and rivets, punches, and drifts. A rack holds more tongs, a stake bickern, and a mushroom stake for forming sheet metals. On the bench at the right of the door are a bar folder for bending light sheet metal, a rod cutter, and an arbor press. In the right foreground appears one end of a four-foot box and a pan brake, for bending sheet steel up to fourteen-gauge thickness.

Bench area.

The Bench Area
Because delicate forging often calls for much filing and fitting, the bench area should be designed so that such work can be done efficiently. At the far left in the photograph, partly shown, is the iron rack for long bars, from which bars can be taken to the bar shear at the far right, to be cut to length. At the left end of the bench hangs a portable punch that can be mounted in the vise for punching holes in light pieces such as H hinges and thumb-latch cusps. On the bench near it is a Beverly shear, an efficient tool for cutting sheet steel, since its design permits cutting curves as well as straight lines. This model works with material to fourteen-gauge; larger models accommodate thicker material. Forming a bench support below it is a set of drawers for storing small tools, patterns, and other material not in daily use. Another set is built into the corner above the bench for similar use. Such arrangements keep tools out of the way and free from rust.

Separating the bench from the show window is a baffle board, which provides privacy while making display space in the window. A two-by-four set on edge with holes drilled in it holds some of the most-used small tools. Here the set of files is within easy reach, with center punches, tap and die wrenches, reamers, and other tools arranged in convenient locations along the line. Since the file is an important tool in finishing small ironwork, there should be an ample selection of both size and type. Here there are round, half-round, flat, and square, in bastard and second cut, from six to sixteen inches in some types. There are times, with large work, when a sixteen-inch file will be the best choice with which to attack a mass of metal. Even with smaller work a longer file often means fewer strokes. When filing H hinge joints, for instance, a square file, being narrower than its equivalent length in a flat one, will fit the joint better and provide the advantage of a longer stroke. Grinding off teeth from one side permits filing a sharp inside corner, required in hinge joints.

A cast-iron surface plate lies on the bench, and on it a steel block for an anvil. The vise is small, with three-inch jaws, ample for small work, of English make, and well built. It is poor economy to try to use a badly constructed vise.

The Bickern
This small stake anvil, perhaps more properly called a beakhorn stake, is very useful for certain purposes, and being portable can be placed where most useful. Although bickerns still may be found in some antique shops catering to tool collectors, few of them will be satisfactory for the sort of work for which this one was made. Its face, heel, and horn are used for small work, but its main function is to provide a series of holes of varying sizes for welding and bearing seating when forging strap-hinge pintles. The holes are slightly oversize, from three-eighths inch to five-eighths inch by sixteenths.

This bickern was forged from two pieces. The top, or working body, was made from an old wagon axle, of steel, two inches square. The ends

The bickern.

were forged under the power hammer, leaving a boss in the center, with its width reduced to one and one-quarter inches. The boss was split with a hot chisel, and opened to a V shape. A piece of wrought iron, one and one-quarter inch square, was forged to a wedge end to enter the V, and welded there to form the stake. A collar was welded to form a shoulder, and the end forged out to drive into the gum stump. Hardening and tempering were not needed, since only very hot iron, and light blows, will touch it.

The Hand Hammer
This is the smith's most versatile tool, for with it he can make many others—chisels, punches, tongs, and swages. Of all forms, for the type of work described in this book, the cross-peen is the most useful, particularly if the smith works without a helper. With it he has two tools in one, a hammer and a fuller. A flip of the wrist changes tools with no time lost to pick up one or the other, while the iron cools and his attention is diverted. Ball-peen and double-faced hammers have their appropriate uses, and will be found in the hammer rack along with the cross-peens.

Smiths may find the size and weight choice of cross-peens limited these days, since ball-peens are more plentiful in greater variety. Converting a ball-peen into a cross-peen is a fairly simple mat-

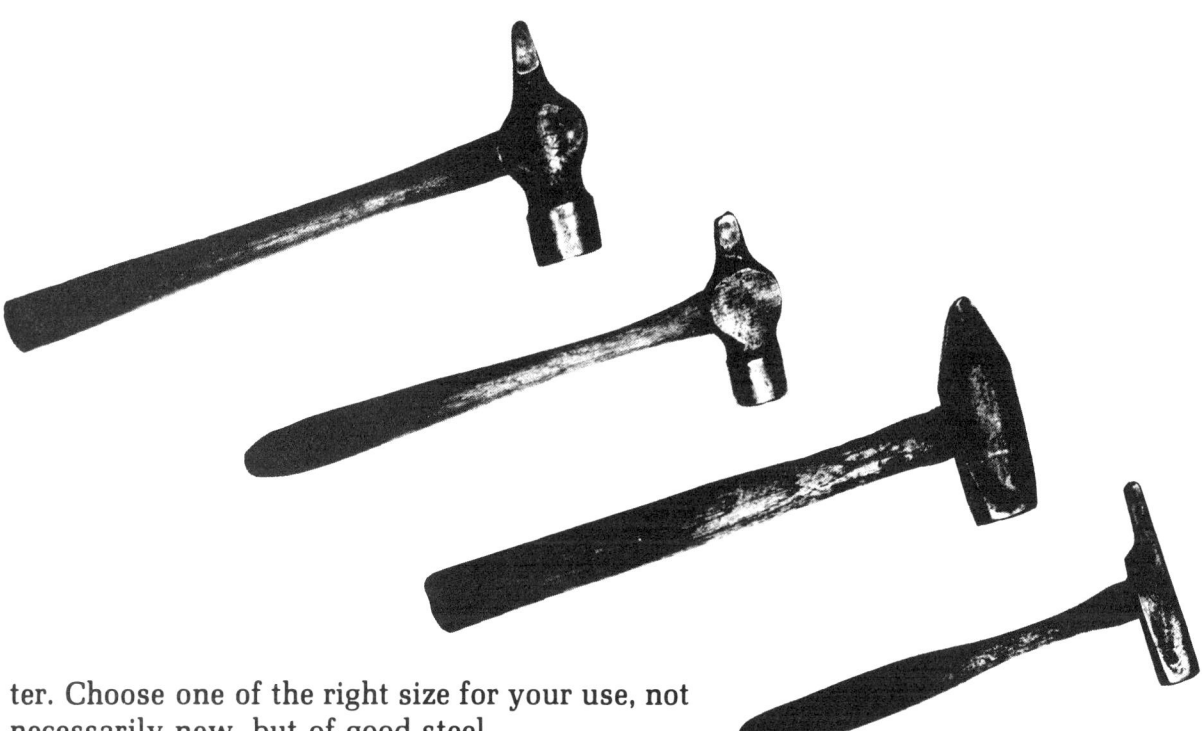

ter. Choose one of the right size for your use, not necessarily new, but of good steel.

In a deep, clean fire, slowly and evenly heat the ball end to orange and forge it to cross-peen shape, squaring the end on the hardy if need be. Then bury it in the ash pile where it can cool slowly until annealed. When cold, file or grind to shape, leaving no sharp edges. It is then ready for hardening and tempering.

Again, at a slow and even heat, bring the whole hammer to a cherry red, since the temper has been drawn from its face during the forging heats. Do not quench it in a bath, which may cool its edges while leaving the center hot, hence soft. Instead, while at the red heat, hold it face up under a stream of lukewarm water from a faucet, allowing the stream to fall on the center of the face and run down over all the edges. This will quench the center, which can barely be too hard. As soon as water stays on the face, polish it with a brick or other abrasive, to show the bright steel. The heat remaining in the body will run to the face and the temper colors will appear. When the oxide is brown, quench it.

Then heat the peen end, cooling the face end as need be to hold its temper. When about an inch of the peen is red, quench a half-inch or so, polish, and draw to a brown. In this way you can provide yourself with cross-peens of any desired weight.

Top to bottom: cross-peen converted from ball-peen, two and one-half lbs.; light forging hammer, one and three-quarter lbs; forging hammer, three and one-quarter lbs; bench hammer, forged from iron with steel face, one and one-quarter lbs.

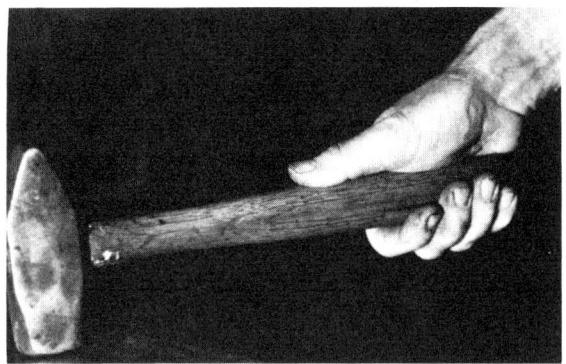

Top, thumb atop handle for flat blow; bottom, thumb at side of handle for angle blow.

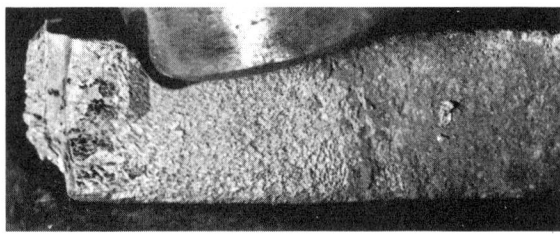

Effect of hammer control, forging a point.

Hammer Control

Most smiths will, out of their experience, find what is for them the best grip to use in swinging the hammer. But since this book deals with hand forging in rather exact ways, the use of the hand hammer should be considered as something more than wielding a chunk of steel on the end of a club. It is because as much time will be taken to heat the iron as will remain in the heat to forge it that "strike while the iron is hot" has any meaning at all. Therefore, a great part of the smith's dexterity lies in his ability to strike the right kinds of blows, in the right places, as quickly as possible.

One key to hammer control is the position of the thumb on the handle. This is not surprising, considering all the other fields of manual skill where rules of thumb literally apply. Whether it is a baseball bat, a golf club, or whatever, the thumb position often dictates the accuracy of the swing. In filing a flat surface, the thumb is placed atop the handle in order to avoid having to control the natural tendency of the wrist to assume that position when otherwise held.

Two basic blows are used in drawing hot iron: that which produces a flat surface parallel to the anvil face, and that which forms a surface at some angle to it. Since it is the face of the hammer which makes the forged plane, accuracy consists of controlling its angle in relation to the anvil top as the hammer descends vertically.

This principle can be demonstrated in a simple forging exercise, that of forging a point on a square bar. Consider that the anvil face is a flat plane of fixed nature. The hammer face is a plane that can assume any angle from horizontal to vertical, and in such position can be driven down into or on hot iron. Logically, if the hammer face is parallel to that of the anvil, the blow will produce a flat surface. However, if the hammer is held at any other angle, and the hot iron is flat on the anvil, the blow will forge a dent or bevel, depending on the placement of the blow. The choice between a flat or angle blow can be determined by the position of the thumb. With the thumb held on the top of the handle, and the wrist held naturally, untwisted, a flat surface will result from a vertical blow. With the thumb moved to either side of the handle, any chosen angle can be forged with equal ease and control.

To forge a point, then, the hammer is held at an angle which is one half of the included angle of the proposed point, the anvil producing the other half, and the bar raised on its end so its axis bisects the angle between them. Vertical blows delivered with one-quarter turns back and forth between them quickly will forge a point at the center of the bar. Because the wrist always holds its natural position, angles remain constant without strain.

This is not to say that this is the only proper way to hold the hammer. It is perfectly possible to produce fine work with all fingers and thumb wrapped around the hammer handle. To roughly reduce stock no such refinement is necessary. But for sustained production of accurate work it is a habit worth acquiring.

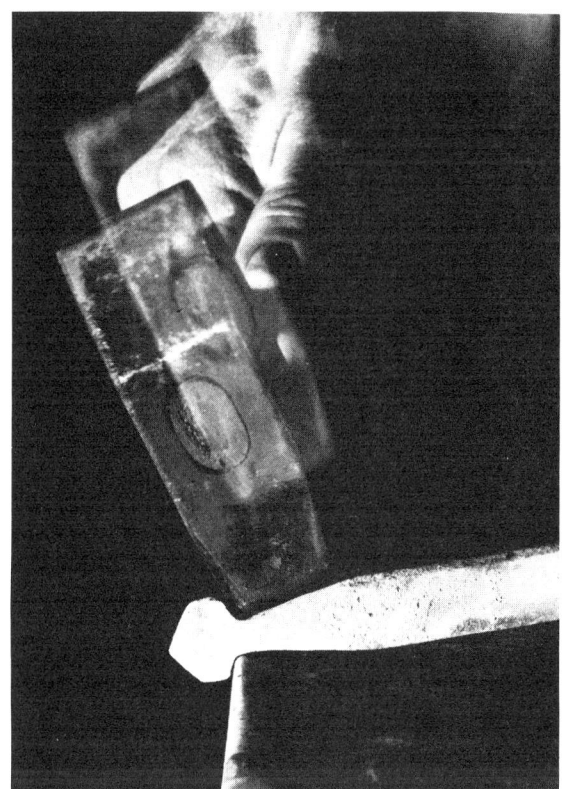

Hammer action, vertical blows forging a neck.

Hammer action, angle blows forging a finial.

Anvil Tools

Smiths make many special tools to use at the anvil, either for a particular job or for general use, by altering stock ones or forging them new. Two of the most useful are a straight-sided hardy and a straight-sided fuller. Both have the effect of leaving a nearly straight or square end on hot iron as it is driven upon them, with a slope only on one side. Handled fullers and hot-cutters can be made to do the same thing, by reforging, and will save upsetting after a cut or fullering to produce a square and sharp outside corner.

Top, anvil die for forging a boss; rough, left, and finished, right, forgings.

Anvil dies and swages for special work.

Special hardy (left) and fullers, and their uses.

Sometimes latch bars must be forged with round bosses at one end, for swiveling in a plate. These are more easily forged in anvil die than filed out cold. Some of these tools are illustrated in use in the text that follows.

The Power Hammer

Some kind of power hammer is a must for any smith who contemplates forging in production rather than one-of-a-kind small ironwork, or who relies upon a helper to strike his handled tools with a sledge. Self-styled purists often object to its use on the grounds that it is not hand forging and not traditional. This is nonsense. Smiths have used power hammers ever since the invention of the waterwheel. The power hammer brings no skill to the work, only energy, and on my scale, skill has a higher value than muscle. One who cannot forge with the hand hammer will do no better with the aid of power, and probably worse. A heavy foot on the treadle can rain a series of mashing blows before the iron can be moved out of the way. Nor is the use of a helper and sledge materially different. Then it is the helper's hands that shape the work, not those of the smith. It is the smith, however, in both cases, who decides how and where each blow should fall. His is the skill, no matter who or what supplies the force.

For small ironwork a power hammer of great size is not necessary. There is little point in having equipment oversized for the work, taking up more floor space and using more energy. The one in this shop is a Little Giant, rated as a twenty-five-pound hammer, which is the weight of the ram. It easily will handle iron up to one-and-one-half-inch diameter, making up to 360 blows a minute. Dies for both fullering and flattening are interchangeable, and special ones can be fitted if desired. The Little Giant is powered by a one-horsepower motor and stands on a three-foot-deep reinforced concrete base. A clutch and treadle regulate speed and thus the force of the blows. It is placed in the shop so that it is handy to both forges, with enough clear space around it to permit operation from the front and two sides.

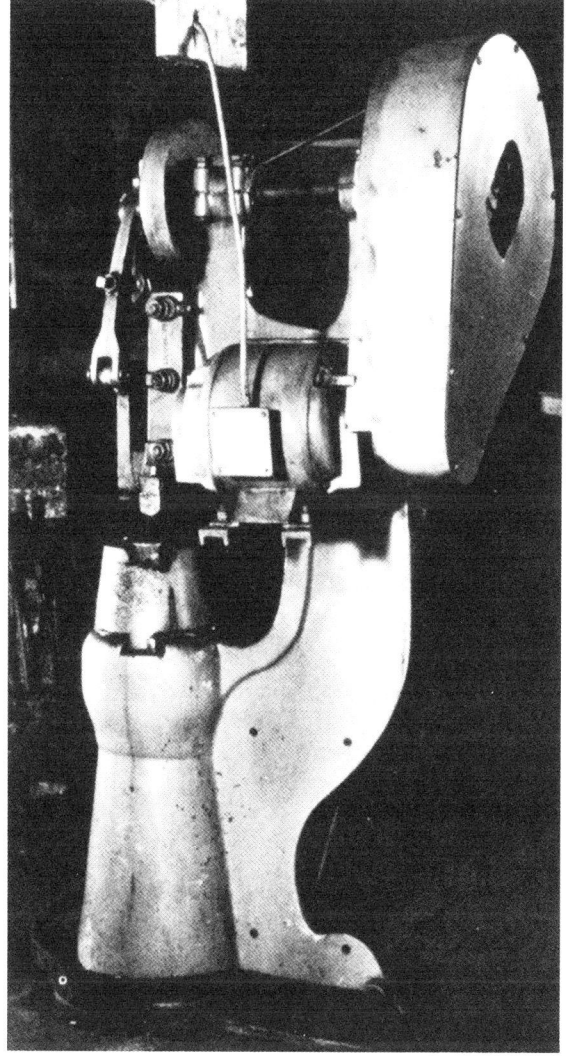

Power hammer.

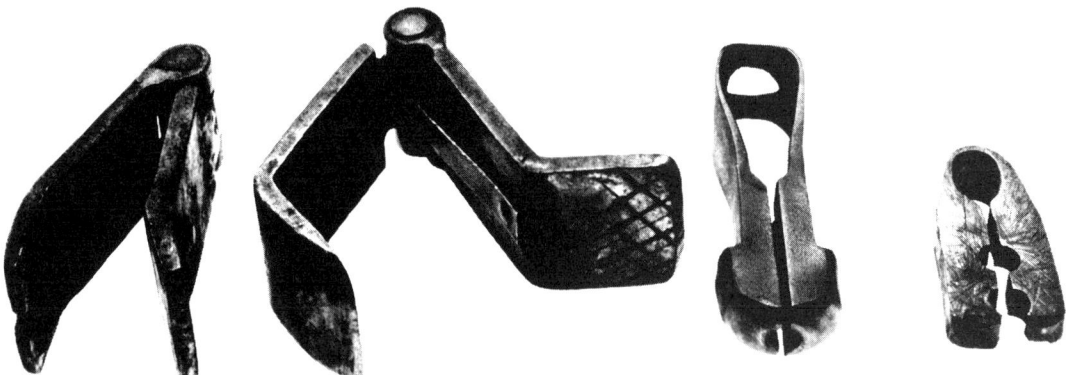

Left, two angle vise clamps; right, two spring clamps.

Bench Tools

Of the many smith-made bench tools, some of the handiest are spring clamps to hold work while filing it in the vise. The angle clamp is simply made, of flat steel, two inches by one-quarter inch, formed into a hinge joint, with hinge leaves of suitable length. The ends of the hinge become the jaws, scored to prevent slipping, beveled at the end for file clearance, and fitted with a flat spring. Jaws are bent to whatever angle suits the work. In this shop there are two such clamps, one bent at about 20° above horizontal, for filing bevels, and the other bent at about 70°, for filing hinge joints and profiles. Both help avoid the need to bend over when at work, and, with natural action, keep all bevels or surfaces at constant angles.

Work that has been dropped in the clamp with the hinge joint down, and is resting in the jaws, can be locked firmly in place by tightening the vise screw. As the screw is loosened, the clamp spring will open to release the work. Such clamps are illustrated in Diderot's Encyclopedia as shop tools used in France in the eighteenth century.

Other forms, simple forged-steel spring clamps

Spring clamp holding work for filing.

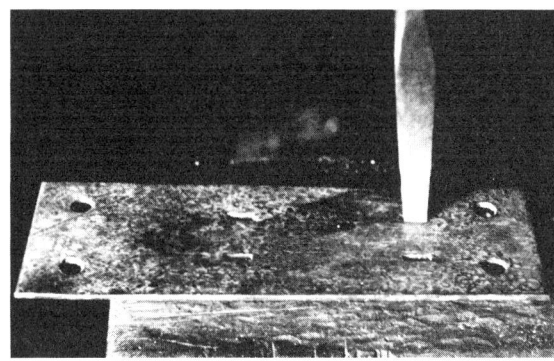

Punching slots over the vise.

with round holes drilled through the centers of the jaws, hold round work when filing or finishing knobs, without scarring the work.

The bench vise itself can be more than a device for holding work. Before the perfection of punches and dies for kick presses, all small slots in sheet metal had to be punched out over the jaws of the vise. In lock and plate-latch work, when only one or two slots are to be made, and parts are to be attached to plates with tenons, it hardly pays to make punches and dies and set up the punch press. In that case the traditional way is the fastest. Slotting punches are made, ground and tempered, of proper sizes. Vise jaws are opened just enough to clear the punch. The slot positions are laid out on the plate, and it is placed on the bench anvil. One or two well-placed sharp blows of the punch mark the positions. This raises up the metal on the other side enough to form a slight ridge, which is the guide for positioning the work over the vise jaws. When properly aligned, the punch is driven through the plate. With proper clearance and care, a clean slot is made. The small amount of burr is easily filed off.

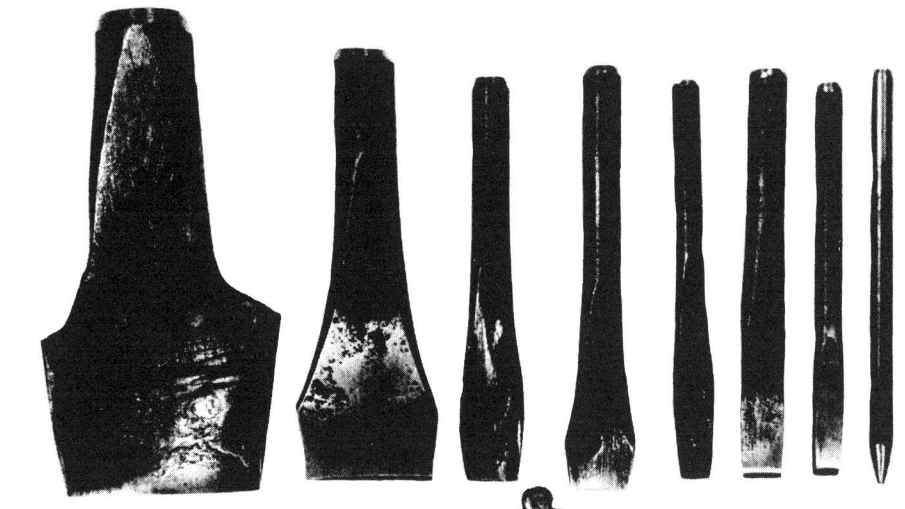

Chasing tools and brass escutcheon.

Chasing tools for striking designs in steel.

Chasing Tools
Once this smith was asked to make some copies of an early eighteenth-century brass escutcheon. The decision was made not to have them cast, with consequent loss of sharp detail, but to make them the way the originals were, by chasing. Tool steel chisels were forged and tempered to match every line element in the design, straight and curved. Because cast brass is not available, and also to distinguish the copy from original work, sheet brass was used. Reproduction should not be faking.

Rivet cutter.

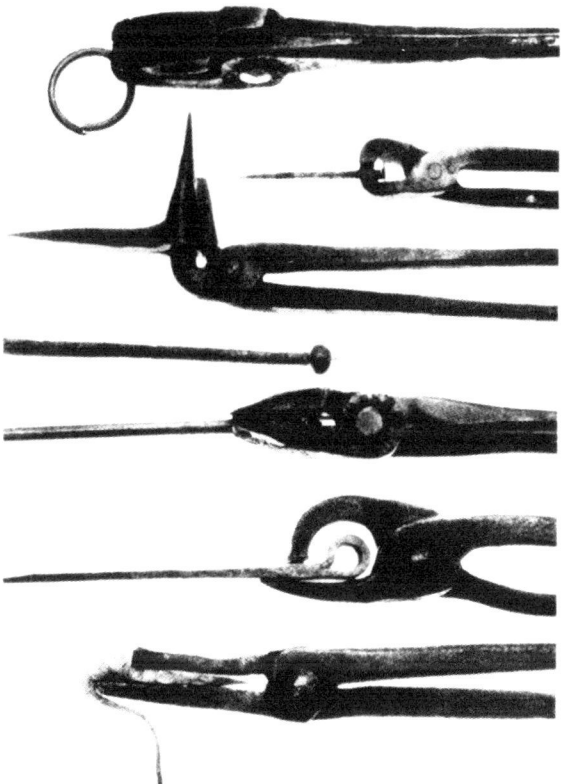

Tongs, altered for special work.

Rivet Cutter

When very short rivets are needed and only longer ones are in stock, they can be cut to the proper length with an expedient tool, easily made. Two pieces of tool steel bar, one short enough to fit in the vise, and the other long enough to provide leverage, are drilled at one end and fitted with a pivot rivet. Quite close to the pivot, with the two pieces lined up together, a hole the size of the rivet to be cut is drilled through both. The top, or handle, is the same thickness as the intended length of the rivet shank.

With the bottom part locked in the vise, just clearing the top of the jaws, the rivet is pushed through the lined-up holes and the handle pulled sharply, neatly shearing off the rivets. Since rivets are soft metal, no hardening or tempering of the cutter blades will be required.

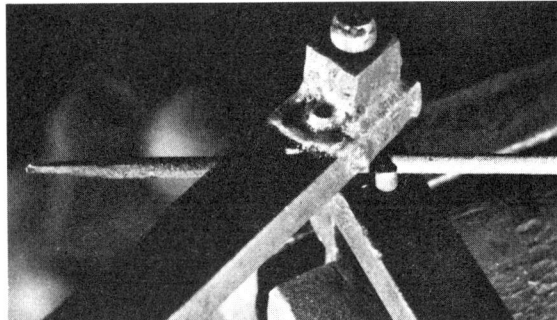

Staple bender, starting the bend.

Staple bent to shape.

Candlestand leg bender.

Staple Bender

Smiths frequently are called upon to make quantities of staples for hooks, pull rings, or the like, of varying wire sizes and lengths. To bend large numbers of such things over the anvil horn is time consuming and inexact. Benders to do this work are quickly made to suit the particular job, then added to the tool supply. A short length of cold-finished round steel of a diameter equal to the inside measure of the staple legs forms a pivot. Short nubs of round stock are riveted through flat bars that form the handles, at a distance from the pivot just wide enough for the wire to lie between them with a little clearance. The height of the nubs should be just a little more than wire size. Small blocks of steel brazed to the handles provide added bearing for the pivot.

In use, the pivot pin is set in the vise. A wire, cut to length and its points forged, is passed between the nubs and centered on the pivot. Movement of either handle will form the bend in its direction, so that visual control is maintained and equality of length easily attained.

Bender for Candlestand Legs

Almost any curve that is an arc of a circle can be bent in a tool that rotates a nose around a center pin, under the same principle that works with the staple bender.

This tool will bend cold steel flat stock, one-quarter inch by one inch, smoothly and without deforming the surface. The bending form itself is made from one-half-inch by one-and-one-half-inch steel, as is the frame and handle, all electric welded together. Pivot pin and rolling nose are one-half-inch-diameter cold-finished steel, with pull rings welded at the ends for easy removal, and oiled for rotation against the work to avoid scraping it.

For forming candlestand legs, one leg at a time is clamped or bolted through a hole in the top of the bed, the pin inserted, and the bend made. The pin is pulled out after bending, to clear the work.

2 PUNCH AND DIE WORK

The Hand Punch

One of the most versatile tools the small ironworker can have in his shop is a hand punch, of the capacity best suited to his work. The punch used in this shop is a Kidder Little Blacksmith, number 35, with a capacity of punching a two-inch-square hole through 16-gauge sheet steel. Although a power punch press is required for mass production, the sort of work described here does not lend itself to the use of such a punch because of the small quantities usually involved. To have tool and die makers produce all the tools one would like to have would be far too costly, and unprofitable. A small hand press is sufficient for the smith who learns to make punches and dies for it.

Working with Tool Steels

This involves working with tool steels, but such study properly is a part of small iron forging on a professional basis, and labor thus spent will pay off many times. The ability to make his own dies places the smith at an advantage over one who must pay someone else to do it for him. Hardening and tempering are not so complicated that they can't be learned by any smith who can forge steel.

Although many tools can be forged from old files with the teeth ground off, old cold chisels, wrecking bars, and the like, the smith often will require tool steel of sizes not found in these sources. For this reason, as well as to insure a stable and known quality of tool steel, he will do well to avail himself of one or more of the many grades of such steel on the market today.

The choice of high-carbon steels is so great that he can choose one that best suits his purposes and equipment, even though he may have no heat-treating equipment except his forge. Most of the punches and dies pictured, for use in the punch press, were made from Bethlehem water-hardening tool steel, grade XCL, carbon range .90 to 1.05 percent. Old smiths would refer to this as steel of 90 to 105 points carbon. Most tool steel manufacturers publish data sheets for each grade of such steel. These sheets are more reliable than any one smith's preference or tradition. They indicate the recommended temperatures for forging, annealing, and hardening, with color equivalents for the temperatures.

Data sheets for Bethlehem water-hardening tool steel show forging temperature at 1800° to 1900°F., with forging stopped at about 1400°. In other words, begin forging at an orange red and quit at a dark red. The quenching temperature is 1425° to 1475°, or between a cherry red and dark red. It is helpful if the quenching bath is warmed to 70° or 90°, to help avoid cracking from too cold a quench. Experience shows the most successful technique.

Once the punch or die has been brought to finish form, it must be annealed, hardened, and tempered. Annealing is done to relieve any strains that may be in the steel from the forging, by allowing it to return to its normal condition of equal softness. With the steel discussed here, this can be done by carefully and slowly bringing it to a dark red to cherry red heat, without raising any scale, and burying it in a pile of ashes, where it can cool slowly without being exposed to drafts of cold air.

To harden, prepare a bath of brine. The saturated solution of salt and water will boil at a higher heat, thus reducing the possibility of steam pockets forming on the steel surface, resulting in uneven quenching. Warm the bath as indicated above. Again bring the piece to a dark red to cherry red heat, slowly and evenly, immerse the work—if a die, completely—and move it about to assure constant cooling, until as cold as the original bath. It then will be as hard as it can get, but far too brittle for use. Only after it has been hardened can it be tempered. Tempering means raising the temperature of the hardened steel, thereby softening it to the desired point for its use.

To draw the temper on a die, first remove the surface oxide with fine abrasive cloth so that the bright steel shows. Heat a bar of steel, a good bit heavier than the die, to a yellow. Place the die upon it, face up, and allow the heat from the bar to penetrate the steel die. As the heat reaches its surface, the temper colors will start to appear, running from light straw yellow, yellow brown, purple, deep to light blue. Move the work about to assure even heat, and when a mid-blue appears, quench the whole in the bath. This method will assure that the under part of the die will be softer than the cutting surface, affording a cushion to absorb some of the thrust shock of the punch.

To harden and temper punches, heat to the quenching color for an inch or so back from the face, and quench only half of that part, holding it vertically in the bath, with agitation. Remove it and polish the face. When the heat behind the face raises its surface to a mid-blue, quench it. If the body of the punch retains enough heat to glow in the dark, do not quench more than the face until it fades out, in order not to harden the shank and make it brittle.

The degree of softness, hence temper color, will depend upon the use to which the tool will be put. Generally speaking, the harder the blow or force used on the tool, the softer it should be, to absorb shock. Thus, heavy cold chisels can be tempered to a light blue, whereas a thin paring chisel, which will be lightly tapped, can be tempered to a dark blue.

Punch and Die Making
Whenever there are many pieces to be made that would be tedious and wasteful of time to file out or cut out with chisels or shears, it will pay to make a punch and die to do the work. After a time, the smith will have a collection of such tools, many of which can be used for other parts as well. Once the smith learns the capacity of the punch,

Shearing cusps of thumb latch in hand punch.

he can make dies and punches to work within it. Round and square ones are not the only kinds that can be used to advantage. Perhaps the most time-saving ones are those that trim forged edges quickly and accurately.

One such tool is a trimming shear blade and die, which is used to cut the profile of rough-forged thumb-latch cusps. The blade is bent so that shearing is done progressively, cutting only a small section at a time. The bed of the die face is cut away so the forged neck of the latch blank can rest in it while that end is being sheared. In use, one side is sheared, the piece turned over to shear the other side, then turned end for end to complete the shearing. Grinding off excess metal in the corners finishes the form. It is now ready to be bent to shape and finish filed.

This principle of making the die to cut only one

Two punches and dies used in combination.

side makes for versatility in the use of the punch, since dies often can be used in combination, one after another, to produce other forms. Sometimes only part of the curve may be needed, to cut.

Here is one example of how more than one punch and die can be used in conjunction. Since the tooling for the second step was already in stock, it was only necessary to make a set to produce the small ogee curve.

First the punch was made, of tool steel, by upsetting the end to form a swelling large enough for the form, and to provide filing clearance past the punch shaft. A lip was left at the far edge of the punch, as a guide, to enter the die before cutting starts, and hold the punch in place. It was sharpened by grinding, then was hardened and tempered.

The die, of annealed tool steel, was roughly filed

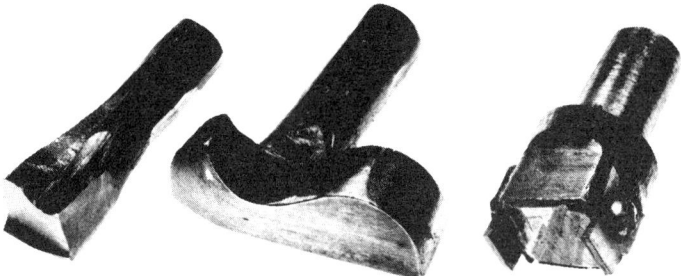

Punches. Left to right: one-piece, two-piece, and three-piece with removable blades.

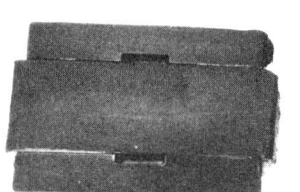

Dies for slotting,

trimming,

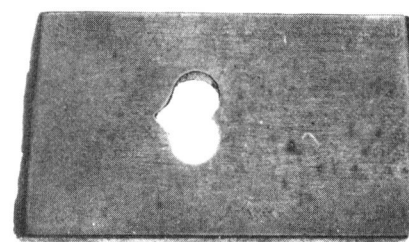

and punching.

to shape, leaving it slightly under size. The guide block for the noncutting sides of the punch was brazed together of mild steel, and it and the die locked in place under the punch. By the use of gradually reducing shims, the tempered punch then was used to trim, little by little, the cutting edges of the die, until they matched. Then the die itself was hardened and tempered.

Only comparatively small punches are best made by upsetting or forging down from larger stock. Larger ones can be made in other ways. Curved shear-blade punches can be cut from one-half-inch flat tool steel and electric welded, at angles to the shaft to produce shear, or bent as shown. Twin slotting punches are needed to punch parallel slots of equal size in bolt plates, to receive the tenons of the staples. These punches can be assembled on a tool steel core with bolts, so they can be replaced when they wear or break.

Dies for small punches can be cut in a single piece of tool steel, drilled, and filed to shape. In all dies, clearance must be provided below the cutting edges, to allow scrap to drop through without clogging the die.

Dies for twin slotters can be made from tool

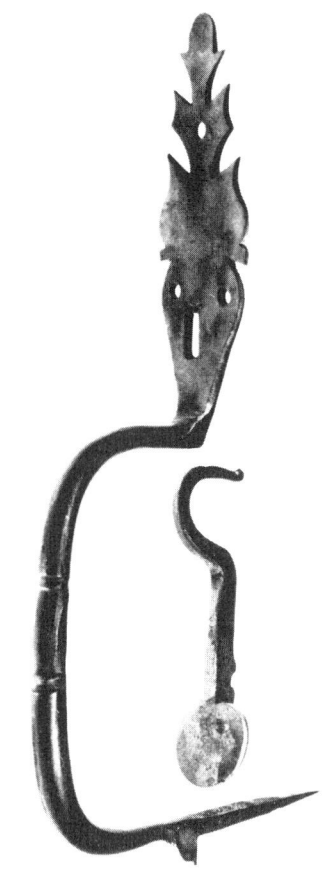

*Thumb latch with
parsley-leaf cusp design.*

steel bars with slots filed in the edges, and a tool steel spacer placed between them. All pieces must be accurately squared, and have sharp edges. The variety of punches and dies that the smith can make is limited only by the capacity of his punch, his needs, and his ingenuity.

Many thumb latches of European origin had very decorative cusps, or finials—survivals, in some cases, of medieval design. One popular eighteenth-century form was the design known as Parsley Leaf, in which a simple ovate leaf form was cut with curved chisels and filed to shape.

To help duplicate this, a double-ended punch and die was made, so that both left and right edges could be punched from the face side, after the latch was bent to shape. A half pattern was cut from thin sheet steel. It was scribed on the surface with a center line as a guide. All of the half-oval notches, and most of the outside curves, can be punched with this tool. Since the profile of the punch has the same curve as a half-round file, only bevel filing is needed to finish the piece. As with other notching punches, a noncutting guide nose in the center of the punch keeps the blades in line with the die as pressure is applied.

Notching the cusp with double-ended punch.

Slotting angle notcher cutting H-hinge blanks.

Notching Punch for Sheet Steel

Hinges that are formed from sheet stock instead of bars, such as H hinges and butterfly hinges, must be cut into blanks before any forging can be done. For this purpose, a notching punch and die is most useful. Since the capacity of the punch press is not sufficient to notch out a corner large enough and thick enough for the purpose, a notcher is made that will do it by means of intersecting slots, thereby countering the resistance of the whole corner.

A two-inch-square mild steel ram is cut to fit the punch channel, with one-half-inch steel plates electric welded to its base, to which blades are bolted. Blades are cut from one-quarter-inch by two-inch tool steel, cut and ground to shear out a right-angled strip the width of the blades. They are butted together at the corner and both cut at the same time, which helps to keep the blank from creeping. Die blades are made from five-eighth-inch by three-quarter-inch tool steel, bolted to a frame, with an adjusting screw to regulate clearance for various sheet thicknesses. All blades are removable for grinding or replacement.

Cold-forming, starting bends in H-hinge eyes.

Pressing H-hinge eyes in arbor press.

Punching cheeks for Norfolk latches.

Cold-Forming with the Hand Punch

In order to save heating time—the most unproductive part of the smith's day—as many operations as possible should be carried out with cold metal. This is particularly true when making H hinges, which require many steps. The hand punch can be used to advantage for this job, since it can be used to form as well as cut.

After the blank is cut for the H hinge, its welding edge is scarfed, and holes are punched for the

Punch and die for slotting Norfolk latch blanks.

joint, to remove most of the material from that part to save filing and sawing, and to reduce tension when making the eye bend.

A round-nosed forming punch is made by brazing to its flat base a piece of drill rod, slightly larger than the finish pin, for ease of fitting. The eye cannot be completely formed in this operation, but it can be started, and with gauges locked in place all similar parts can be started alike.

To complete the bend, ready for welding, a jig is made for use in the arbor press, which allows more travel than the hand punch. The jig is a section of angle steel with ears welded along two edges, projecting past the sharp corner of the angle. An assembly pin, dropped in the channel formed by the forming punch, is held in place by the ears as the ram closes the joint. Two positions are required to close it down flat, after which a thin chisel opens the joint for fluxing at the weld.

3 <u>WHITESMITHING</u>

FLESH FORK

During the centuries when all cooking was done over an open fire, smiths were called upon to make all sorts of tools and utensils for fireplace use. One such implement essential to much food preparation was the flesh fork, used for turning meat on the grill, for toasting bread, and for other purposes. Such forks occurred in great varieties of size and design. They were made, on occasion, by village smiths with a light enough touch, but for the most part by whitesmiths or cutlers in the urban centers, who usually worked from templates and standard designs.

Because tools used with food must be kept clean, they must be forged much smoother than ironwork not so used—but not for this reason alone. The whitesmith's work was as concentrated at the bench as at the forge. He well knew the truth of the rule of thumb that ten minutes at the forge saved two hours at the bench. So he finished his forgings at a heat low enough not to raise a scale; for it is the scale, pounded into the iron's surface, that takes tedious time to file out.

The whitesmith was no less skilled than the blacksmith. Indeed, he was probably more so, from the nature of his work. His name describes him as the blacksmith's does him. Since he spent less time at the smoky forge, he didn't get so black.

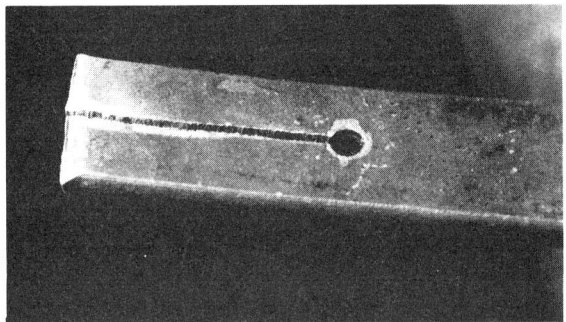

Top, punched and sawed; bottom, ends opened into a Y.

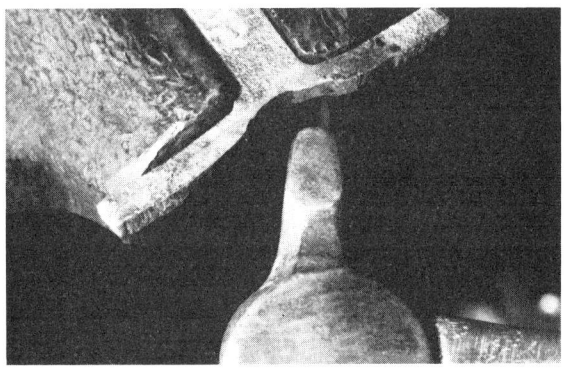

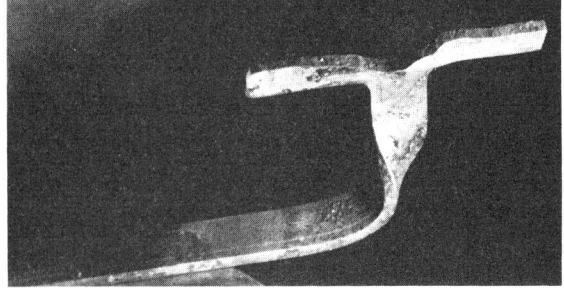

Top, making the T bend; bottom, the twist.

The making of a fine flesh fork, then, requires a little more discipline than making a simple strap hinge, which can be practically finished at the forge. For the one illustrated here, soft steel, three-sixteenths inch by three-quarter inch, of suitable length, is used. Drill or punch a three-sixteenth-inch hole two inches from one end, and saw down the center of the flat from the end to the hole. At a yellow heat, bend the edges outward into a wide Y, but do not bend them to sharp right angles.

The next step is critical, and if not carefully done will mar the following work without being noticed until too late. It is good practice to avoid sharp inside corners at this point, since the danger is that the metal, driven back upon itself, will fold over and form a hot shut. It may not be apparent, but a crack then exists at that corner, which will open as the tines are brought to their shape. One way to avoid this is to grind the corners of the jaws at one end of the vise on a radius to remove the sharpness. With the iron at a yellow heat, hot enough to give time to position the work without critical heat loss in the cold vise, lock it in place, and with the cross-peen gently nudge the iron around the curve of the jaw to a right angle. Use light blows to avoid reducing the stock size below what will be needed for the tines.

Left, forging the tines; right, starting the round neck.

Remove the work from the vise and forge the split so that the tines lie in a straight line across the bar, with a very shallow curve at the center.

Take another heat and drop the T-shaped end into the vise, an inch or so below the end of the T, and make two 90° bends, one flatwise and one edgewise, so that the tines are parallel to the line of the bar and along its center line. You now can forge one of the tines without the trouble of holding the work at an angle. Forge the tine to a square-tapered point, then round it. Record its length on the anvil with soapstone or in some other way. Reverse the flat bend and forge the other tine to match the first. If they are not the same length, cut or draw one or the other until they are. If the saw did not run true in the center, there may be more stock in one than the other, and now is the time to equalize them. Straighten out the bends to the original flat bar. One of the conveniences of forging iron is that it can be bent out of the way on occasions like this and restored to its former shape with little effort.

Heat and bend the tines into their curve. Place the fork end so that it projects over the far edge of the anvil, leaving just about an inch of the bar stock intact. Hold the hammer at an angle as previously described, and forge one end of what will be

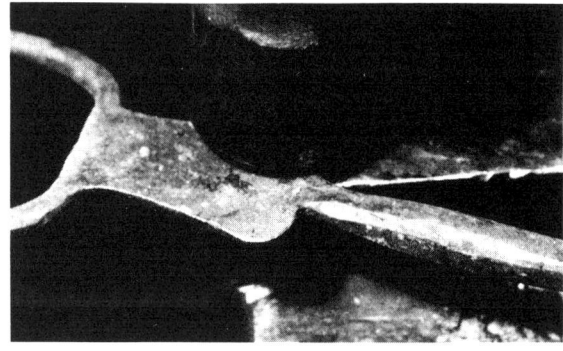

Top, thinning the flat neck; bottom, flaring the curve.

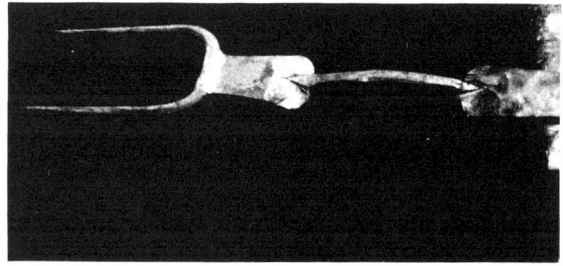

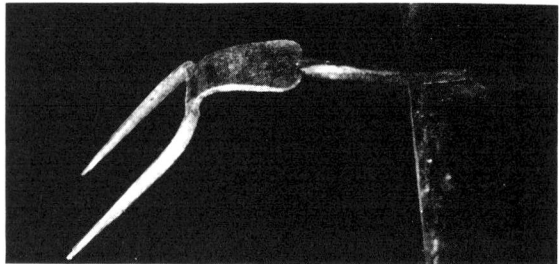

Top, the reinforcing Vs; bottom, starting the bend.

the round section between fork and handle. Forge it to a square taper about an inch long. Then, holding the work so that the curved tines are over the anvil table, protected from false blows or hammer shock, forge the other square taper. Then round the whole section, leaving it thicker in the center.

Since three-sixteenth-inch stock is thicker than needed here, hold the piece with the curve of the tines projecting past the far edge of the anvil, and reduce the thickness to a shy one-eighth inch at that point, tapering back to full thickness at the round part, so that the full thickness of the tines continues through the whole curve.

With the fork held over the edge of the anvil again, this time at an angle, forge down the thick part next to the round section by drawing it sideways, producing a curved edge while leaving a thicker, tapered section at the center of the underside, reinforcing the transition between the two. Forge the other side to the same curve.

Treat the handle section in the same way, providing the same transition form, and thinning it to just under one-eighth inch, tapering to narrower width at the end. Cut from the bar and forge a thin, tapered tongue at the end to form a scrolled hanging hook. Clean the anvil of scale and finish forge

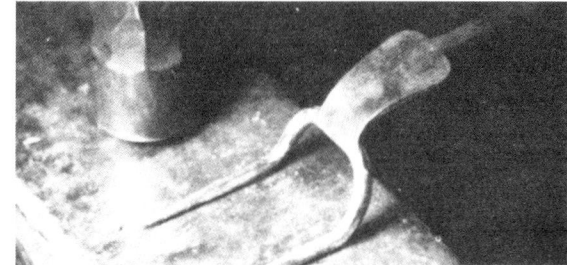

Left, bending the legs; right, finishing the form.

at a red heat, striking first on the edges to crack off any scale. Forge with the face of the work on the anvil to avoid the marks of hammer blows. The forging is now complete. All that remains is bending and finishing.

Make the first bend in the flat behind the tines. This is the proper place, not only for utility, but also to strengthen the flat at that place. Then bend the tines one at a time until they match and curves are smooth. Rest it in the anvil on end to see that it stands upright on the points, and sight down it to find any twist. Bend the hanging hook. The fork is now ready for finishing, and if carefully forged, scale will be minimal.

This is where whitesmithing techniques come into play. Since what forging scale persists is harder than the metal beneath it, time and file teeth can be saved by first removing it. Immerse the whole in a bath of acid such as mercuric, which is readily available at builders' supply houses. Leave it there long enough to dissolve the scale, but not so long as to pit the surface. Immediately rinse it thoroughly in very hot running water and bury it in a box of powdered lime, moving it about to dry it completely. This will neutralize the acid and passivate the metal.

In the angle vise file the edges to their final

outlines. A piece of cardboard placed beyond the vise helps to screen out whatever is on the bench and allow the eye to concentrate on the profile of the work.

While the handle remains unfinished, dress the tines, filing so that they are nicely rounded and all curves are smooth. Use copper or plastic jaw covers in the vise to prevent scarring surfaces, and file the flat surfaces, first with a coarse and then with a fine-toothed file. Holding the file crosswise of the work, grasping it at both ends, drawfile with several strokes. This will highlight the places where much metal must be removed in order to get down to a clean and true plane. If any rather deep hollows exist, they often can be raised by hammering on the back on a smooth anvil. After removing excess stock and correcting any dents, drawfile to a plane surface. Drawfiling should continue until no scratches or dents remain, and no wavy sections catch the light. As one surface is finished, protect it with a few layers of masking tape to keep out iron filings.

After all surfaces are finished, the bevel decoration and chasing can be done, with half-round fine files and chasing tools made for the purpose. File the bevels almost to the bottom edge, but do not alter the profile. Soften all edges with fine abrasive cloth. Warm the fork to drive out moisture, and coat it with a good hard paste wax.

KITCHEN LADLE

The forging of a kitchen ladle involves some of the same steps used in making a flesh fork and a fire shovel (see page 60). The handle is similar to that of the fork, and the bowl is started in the same way as the shovel, but with lighter material.

Forge the blank for the bowl from a piece of flat stock, one-quarter inch by two inches. Neck it in to form a throat, and weld it to the handle stock, which is three-sixteenths by three-quarters, the same as the fork handle. Sizes depend upon the design you intend to follow.

Use a fuller with a striker, a heavy cross-peen hammer, or a power hammer to widen and thin the blank. Using repeated yellow heats, but avoiding burning as weight lessens, do the final stretching over the horn of the anvil, then flatten the blank over the anvil.

When the blank is thinned to slightly more than one-sixteenth of an inch, and as smooth as the hammer will leave it, use dividers to scribe a circle of desired size, and trim the edges. If any substantial unevenness appears, reforge and re-trim.

In the absence of a swage block with ladle forms, some expedient is helpful in starting to sink or to raise the bowl. For this smith, years of scrapyard scavenging have yielded a hollow cast-iron cap from some sort of valve or pipe fitting, and a heavy round cast-iron weight with conveni-

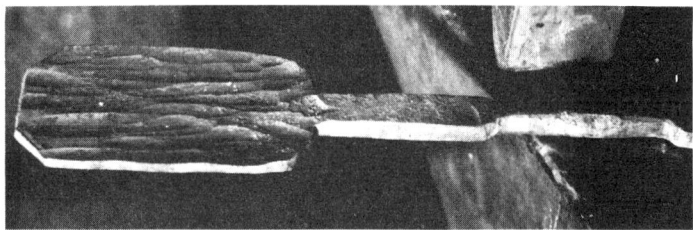

Top, bowl and handle blanks welded; bottom, fullering the bowl blank.

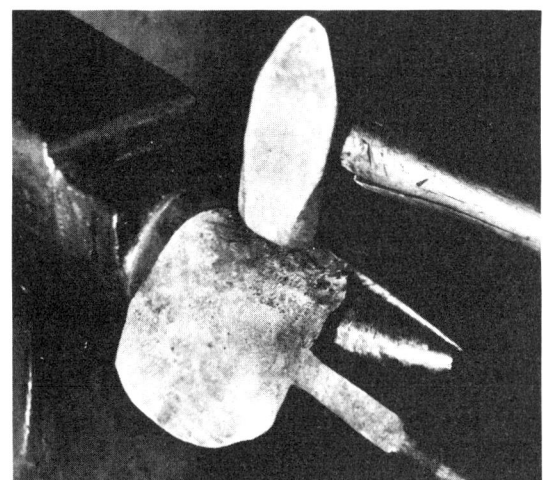

Thinning the bowl blank.

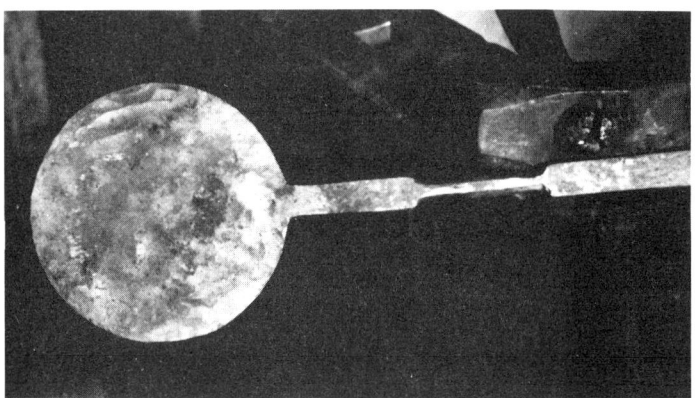

Bowl blank cut to shape.

Starting the bowl form.

Planishing the inside with the hammer.

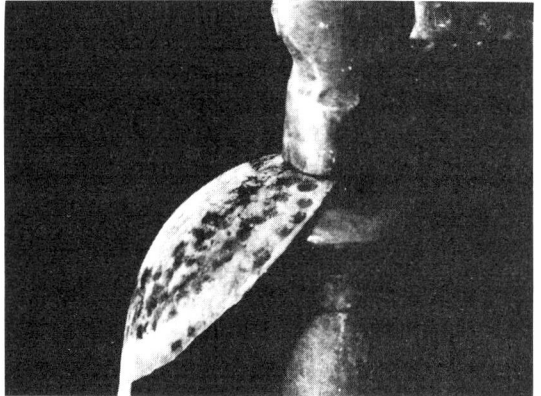

Planishing the outside on a mushroom stake.

ent holes for holding, which fits rather neatly in the pipe cap. With the bowl heated red, the weight presses it into the iron mold and starts the bowl. Action is repeated until full depth is reached, hammering out wrinkles as they appear, with an old hammer whose face has been reshaped into a shallow curve.

Whether you use an expedient such as this or a swage block, when scale flakes off into the mold, remove it between steps to avoid pounding it into the surface of the work.

When you have roughly finished the bowl, forge the handle in the same way as the flesh fork, or to your own design. Then descale the piece for finishing, as for the fork.

There may be pits in the inside surface of the bowl. Since they cannot be filed out, use a mushroom stake or other convex steel or iron form, polished smooth, to remove them. Moving the bowl around on it, hammer the outside until all dents or bumps blend into a smooth surface.

Initial surfacing of the inside can be done on a fine grinding wheel, faced in a curve, and of the right diameter. Final polishing in this case was done in the drill press, with strips of fine emery cloth wrapped around an etcher's ink dauber. Other expedients will occur to you. Many polishing attachments are available or can be made. Abrasive cloth glued to a doorknob fitted to a shaft is one example.

The outside of the bowl presents no problem. It can be smoothed on a sanding belt, but a pneumatic rubber polishing head is more satisfactory. The pneumatic head is resilient because of the air inside it, which can be varied in pressure. Curved surfaces can be finished with fewer flats.

Grinding the inside on curved abrasive wheel.

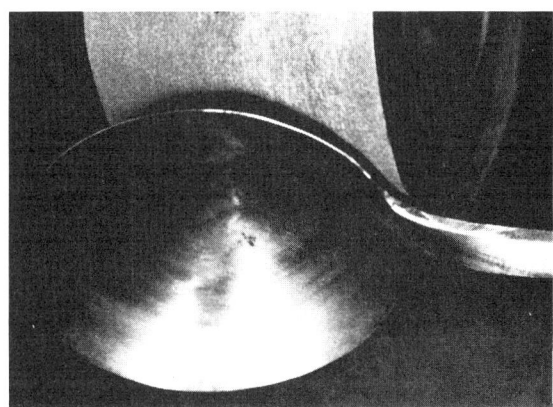

Smoothing the outside on the sanding belt.

Polishing the inside on the drill press.

SWIVEL TOASTER

This early eighteenth-century hearth toaster, simpler than more ornate forms, was easier to clean but not necessarily easier to make. Although some styles were constructed of many elements, here the whole cage was forged from one bar. No twists or scrolls attract the eye, which sees at once the unity and utility of the piece. The cage will accept old-fashioned hearth loaf slices up to seven inches wide and one inch thick—quite evidently made for hearty eaters. It turns on a pivot to toast both sides.

To make the cage, cut a piece of flat steel three-sixteenths inch thick and one and one-half inches wide, eleven inches long, and mark its center. From the center, at two and one-quarter inches to each side, drill quarter-inch holes and shear to them on center from each end. Bending one out of the way, forge each end out into a strip edgewise, increasing in width and length and decreasing in thickness from the main body, to eight inches long from the center mark. Keep the outside edges straight. This will increase the span between the strips. Check to see that all are the same in cross-section.

File the inside curve at each end to a smooth seven-sixteenths-inch radius and trim all ends to

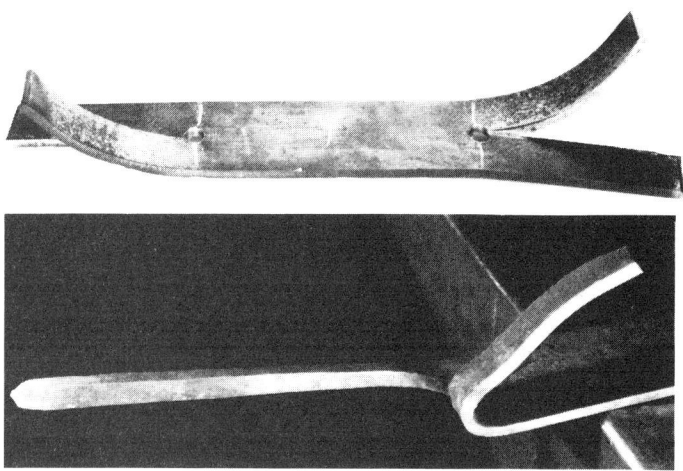

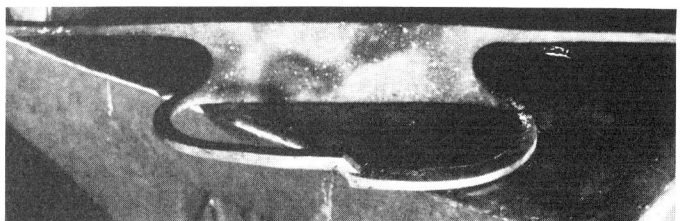

Top, blank punched and slit; bottom, starting the forging.

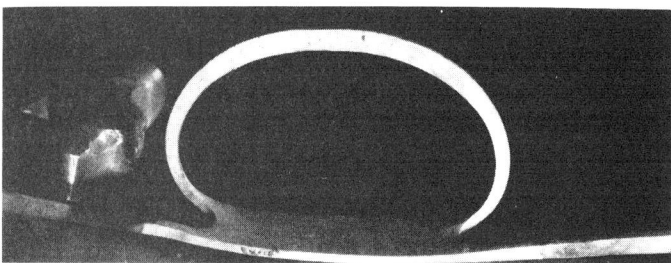

Top, the first weld; bottom, curve completed.

the same length. Now file all surfaces to disclose any irregularities that need to be corrected, and reforge where necessary. This will be easier to do now than after the bends are made.

Scarf the ends for lap welding, and bend the strips over the horn so that they join at the top of the curve. The lap is made not on the scarf slope, but with the flat sides together. This has the advantage of helping to make a smoother weld in this rather thin material, since none of the welding surfaces will be in contact with the anvil, which may cool them. Also, this will make a shorter weld and will cut down the welding time.

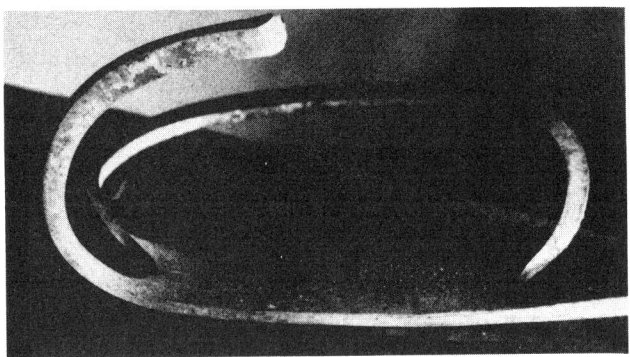

Left, first side bent over; right, the cage completed.

It is the thin ends of the scarf that cool first, and this method insulates them from that danger.

Correct the balance in the curve, and finish file the surfaces exposed to welding heat. Heat the piece so that only the bottom parts of the curve are red, to protect the form already established, and bend the welded loop over out of the way so the other half may be welded. Proceed to form and weld the other side of the cage. Finish file it, and bend the first one into its proper position. Then carefully equalize the curves in each side until they match.

The stand consists of handle, front legs, and back leg. For the front legs, use a bar three-sixteenths inch by one-half inch by eight and one-half inches. Mark the center. Leave full thickness there, and reduce the rest to one-eighth inch thick, keeping the original width. Forge the handle from three-sixteenths-inch by three-quarter-inch material. Scarf the cage end for a T weld and the center of the front leg piece.

Forge the center section into a rectangular form at right angles to the flat top. Thin the handle end to one-eighth-inch thickness, with a thin taper at its tip to form the rat-tail loop for hanging and for easy handling. The total length of the handle, not including the rat-tail part, should be about ten and one-half inches before welding. Make the T weld.

From the center of the weld, trim each leg to five inches and flare the end to form a slight scroll for a

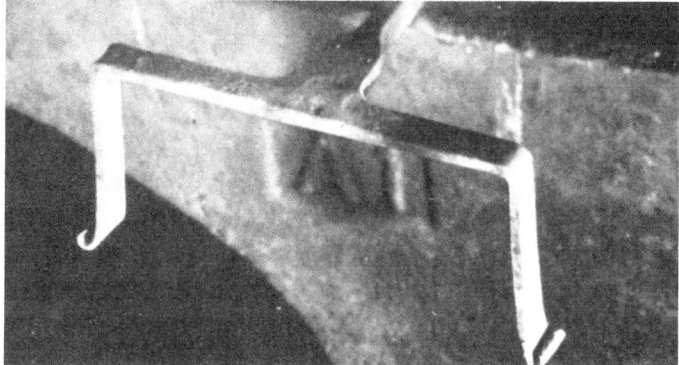

Top, handle welded to legs; bottom, legs bent, feet scrolled.

foot. Bend at slightly less than right angles at two and one-half inches from the end of the scroll, so that each leg is somewhat splayed. Forge the back leg from one-quarter-inch by three-eighth-inch stock and flare and scroll its foot. At a height to set the toaster level, file a tenon and drill or punch a hole in the front part of the flat handle section to fit it. Countersink the top of the hole for flush riveting. Form the rat-tail end.

Descale all parts and drawfile all surfaces. Rivet the back leg into place and file down its top to blend with the handle surface. Forge a quarter-inch rivet with a generous oval head and file it smooth. Drill oversize quarter-inch holes in the center of the cage base and center of the front legs. Make a thin washer to go between them, for clearance when turning, and rivet all together so as to move easily but not too loosely.

RUSH LIGHT WITH BOX JOINT

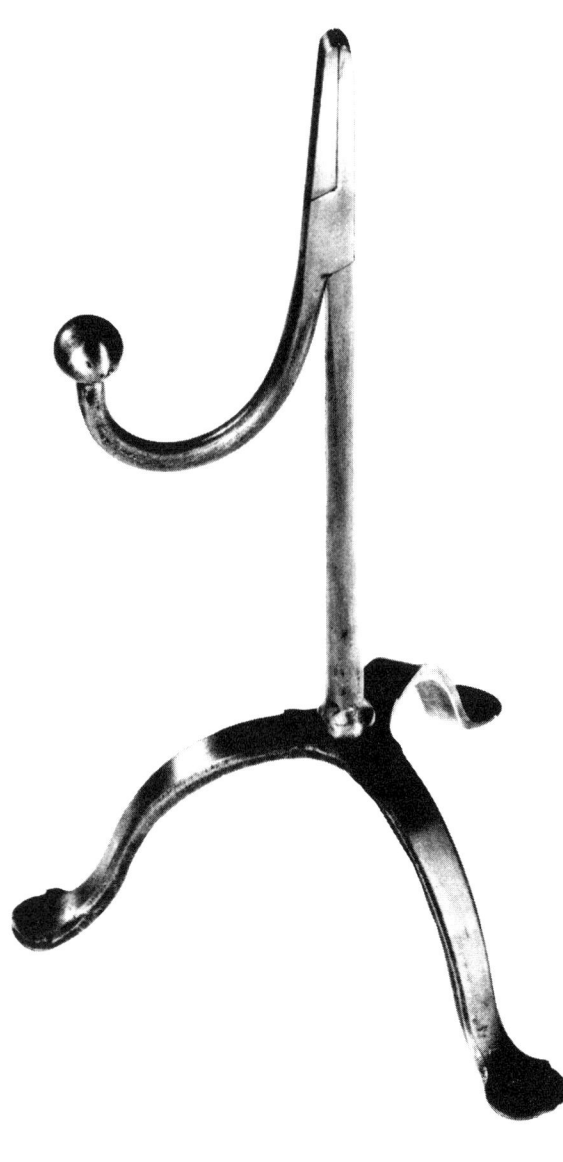

The box joint was used by eighteenth-century whitesmiths and cutlers in making instruments and tools where the jaw action must be true and unaffected by the natural side pressure of thumb and fingers. Side pressure is necessary in scissors in order to squeeze the two cutting edges together, which is why they are made for both right- and left-handed users. Side pressure is not necessary, however, in sugar nippers, curling irons, and some surgical instruments, where accurate alignment of the working ends is critical. Occasionally some fine rush lights were made using the box joint. Instead of a plain lapped joint, the male part of the box joint passes through the center of the female. It is supported through its whole movement in constant alignment.

The rush light shown here is rather dainty—suitable for a lady's chamber. It stands only nine and one-half inches high, with a base radius of three and one-quarter inches.

Forge the uprights from seven-sixteenths-inch-square mild steel. Starting at the end of the bar, forge the jaw down to three-sixteenths inch thick and three-eighths inch wide, tapering to slightly less at the tip. Reduce the joint section to three-eighths-inch thick, which will widen it enough to give stock to file down to finish size. Forge the shanks to a full five-sixteenths inch round, leaving one-half inch of full stock at the end to form the knob on one and the collar and stud on the other cut from the bar. Don't try to finish forge them until the joint is fitted. If that fails, all other labor will be wasted.

File the flat faces of the joints, and coat them with dark marking ink. Punch a mark in the center of the joints. From the punch marks scribe arcs which will just escape inside and outside corners. At a tangent to the edges of the arcs, scribe lines to the inside corners. File off the outside corners to the scribed lines and file the insides of both jaws, so that when placed over each other in closed position they will clear.

The arc is the line of travel of the outside corner of the male part. Any material left inside the arc on the female part will cause obstruction. Any material cut away from the arc on the male part will cause a gap. Square across the edge of the male part, and lay out tangent lines to match those on the other side. From a center line on the edge, lay out one-eighth inch for the thickness of the joint. Saw carefully along the tangent lines to slightly less than finished depth, indicated by your layout lines. Cut in two directions across the joint, leaving small studs. With a sharp, small, cold chisel carefully cut off the studs on both sides. They will offer little resistance, so you will not need to use hard blows that might damage the joint.

Using a file with one safe edge, file the joint to finished size, taking care that both sides are alike and square with each other to assure proper fit.

Place the male part on the female part in closed position and square across the edges, marking the ends of the filed portion of the male on the edges of the female. Lay out a slot one-eighth-inch wide connecting these marks. Draw a center line through the slot mark. Drill three-thirty-second-inch holes along the line, clear through where possible without spoiling the slot, and at angles intersecting them, to remove as much metal as possible. The steel may be cut hot, if you choose, but the risk of spoilage is greater. Cold working is more accurate. Since no great amount of material must be removed, it will not be tedious.

With a narrow flat punch, knock out the ridges left between the drilled holes. Forge a narrow cold

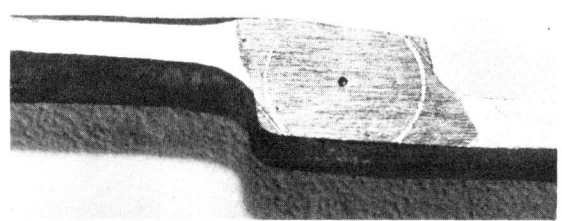

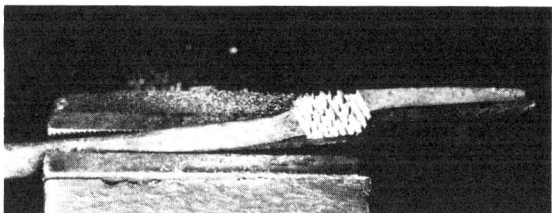

Top, laying out the male part; bottom, sawing the joint.

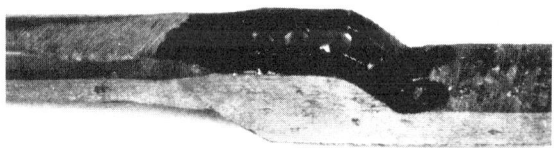

Starting the female joint.

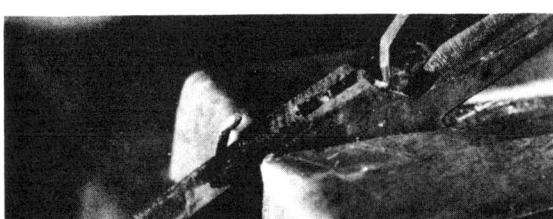

Top, clearing the slot; bottom, filing to fit.

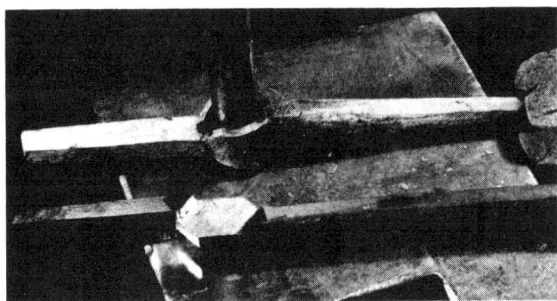

Top, expanding the slot; bottom, parts ready for assembly.

chisel, a little less than one inch wide, with the bevel ground edgewise at a sharp angle. Harden and temper it to a dark blue. Use it to pare away the metal to clear the slopes and leave sharp corners in the slot.

Since there is no accurate way of knowing if the male part will fit the slot through which it must pass, make a template by filing a piece of steel to the same size as the male part. Use a thin warding file and file the slot until it fits.

With the joint ready, the shafts can be forged to final shape. Forge the knob and collar from the lumps at the ends of the shafts.

To join the two shafts, heat the female part to a red heat. Using a series of tapered round punches of increasing size, enter the slot and gently spread its walls apart, working from both sides and heating evenly. Do not overheat or strike too hard. The idea is to bend the walls, not to stretch them. Try the hole with the male part. When it just clears in the open position, take another heat, insert it, and gently hammer down the open slot and close it, again working from both sides. If all has gone well, it will fit snugly in the slot, yet move freely as it should. Since the forging is still pretty full and rough, any gaps can be closed by light hammering.

Drill a one-eighth-inch hole in the center of the joint and fit with a trial rivet. If the joint is tight, heat it and work loose, or stretch it. The trial rivet is used so that if the pin should bind, by one part stretching against it, or be bent, it can be drilled out and a new, larger hole made. Once the joint is safely made, the work can be descaled and finish filed. It is ready for the base.

To make the base, use one-quarter-inch by three-quarter-inch stock. Make a 180° bend three inches from the end, and cut from the bar three

The joint completed.

Drawfiling the base in the angle vise clamp.

inches from the center of the bend. Leaving the bend at full thickness, thin the legs to three-sixteenths inch, tapering to five-eighths inch wide at the ends. Scarf the bend for a T weld and weld another piece of similar stock to it for the third leg. Try the angles on a template, or protractor, and cut and forge the welded leg to the same section and length as the other two. Flare the ends of the feet into penny form and thin the legs behind them in transition taper. Choose the better side of the weld, if there is one, for the top face. At a red heat, hammer it face down on the anvil.

Descale it and finish file all profiles and surfaces, using the angle vise clamp. It is better to do this before bending, since it will be easier to produce true planes. Heat it to red and bend all legs, either over the horn or on a form made for that curve. Descale again, polish, and attach the base, with the counterweight standing over one leg for stability.

PIPE TONGS, AMERICAN

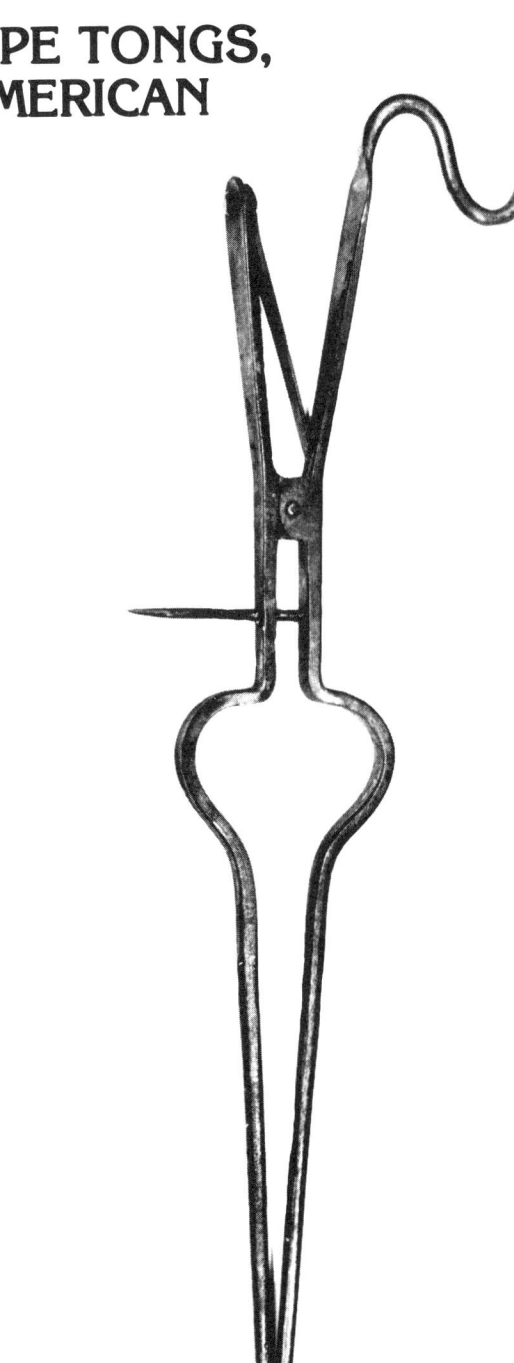

Gentlemen smokers in colonial days sometimes used tongs of this type to light their pipes. The pair shown here is a simple traditional American form, quite free in design and lacking some of the exactness and finish of professional English work of the same period. The spring-loaded tongs can be used to pick up and hold a hot coal from the hearth fire and place it on the tobacco in the pipe. The small disk at the end of the curved tail serves as a tamper. The spike near the middle of the tongs not only keeps the legs aligned, but also can be used to ream out the bowl. Such implements often rested on the mantel shelf or hung on a nail nearby.

Pipe tongs show a great variety of design. Some pieces exhibit exquisite craftsmanship and individual taste. Some of the finer ones may have been made by English whitesmiths who settled here, or by gunsmiths or locksmiths, either of whom would have had the requisite skill to produce them. Since few craftsmen signed their ironwork in those days, the makers are seldom identified. Surviving originals command fabulous prices in the antiques market, and differences in finish and detail may account for variations in price. The pair shown here, which is eighteen inches long, is comparatively rough when compared with the English pair that follows.

To make these tongs, use half-inch-square iron or steel. Draw out two pieces to eleven inches, tapering from about three-sixteenths inch by seven-sixteenths inch down to seven-thirty-seconds inch square. Leave small lumps at the ends to form disks, and sharp inside and outside cor-

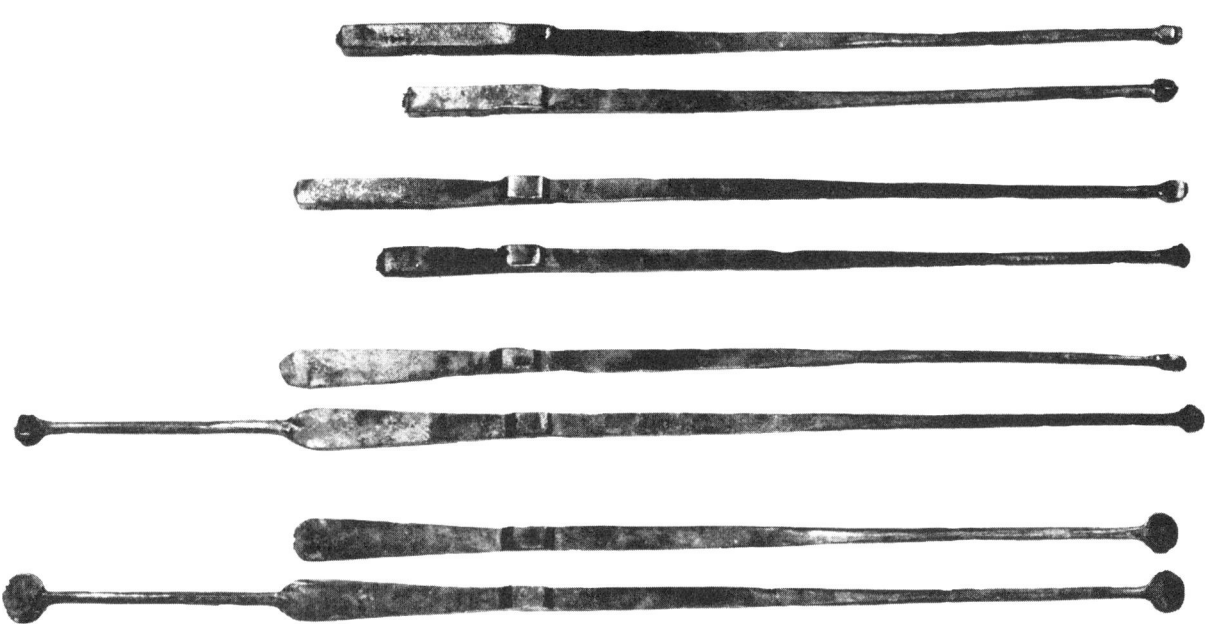

Top to bottom, steps in forging the parts.

ners where the forging begins. Cut off from the bar leaving two inches of square stock for one piece and three inches for the other.

Now round the small square leg sections, reducing to equal length and section, and forge flat sections on the other ends for handles, leaving three-quarter inch of square stock for the joints. Forge the shorter piece first to provide a template for forging the other handle section. From the point of equal handle length, forge a round section with a lump at its end for the tamper, about five inches long overall. Leave a reinforcing section from handle to tail, as was done with the flesh fork. Handle sections will be flared at the ends, and taper from three-sixteenths inch at the joint to under one-eighth inch at the ends. Finish the rough forging by forming all the disks.

The next step is to prepare the joint. Start by heating the bosses left from the forging, white hot. Set each boss in the vise and squeeze the jaws tight to reduce the width. Sharpen the inside corners by hammer blows on the top.

To make the female part, split the boss down

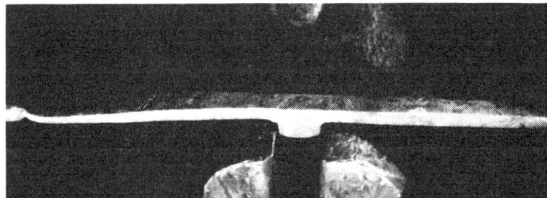

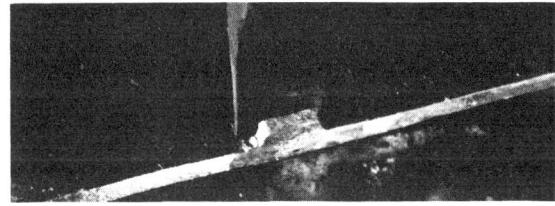

Top, squaring and upsetting the boss; bottom, splitting the female joint.

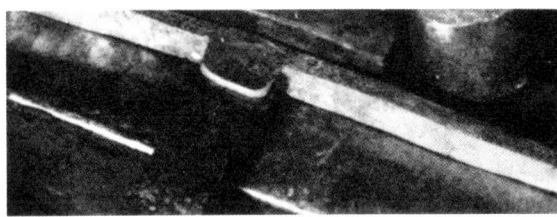

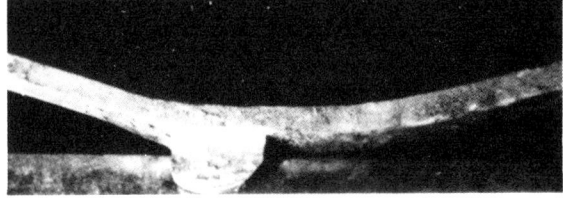

Top, dressing the female joint; bottom, forging the male.

Left, jig for angle bend; right, jig for the leg curve.

the middle with the hot chisel to the level of the flat section, taking care to see that the blade is centered and vertical, to produce equal sides. Then prepare a forging plug, or mandrel, one-eighth inch thick by three-quarter inch wide, and two or three inches long. Grind its end on a curve that is a radius from the center of the joint, and drive it into the slot so that it penetrates the flat section. This will provide clearance for the male part, which will be similarly curved. Take another heat, turn the piece sidewise against a swage or other anvil tool base to hold it in place, and forge the joint down flat, reducing thickness and increasing width to some degree. Work from both sides to equalize the thicknesses.

To make the male part, curve the piece slightly so that only the part to be forged rests on the anvil, at its edge, and forge the boss down to one-eighth inch thick. Center the piece. File out the corners while it is still bent. Straighten the leg and handle.

File and fit the joint so that it moves freely. Drill a one-eighth-inch hole in its center and fit with a trial pin. When it moves properly, file all surfaces neatly. Drawfile all flats and the faces of the pick-up disks and round sections. Final profiles of the disk ends can await final assembly and proper alignment.

Bends can be made from chisel or center-punch marks measured from the pin, but if you plan to make more than one pair or duplicate the form at a later time, it will pay to make jigs for these operations. Curves and angles will match more closely, and much time will be saved.

Two jigs are needed, one for making the sharp bend, and one for forming the curve in the legs. To make the angle jig for the sharp bend, use a piece of one-quarter-inch by one-inch steel, ten inches long. Saw two slots edgewise, five-eighths inch deep, one at two inches from the end and the other at three inches. At a yellow heat, in the vise, forge the part between the saw cuts over at a right angle and thin it to one-eighth inch. At its center cut a slot one-eighth inch wide into which the trial pin will fit snugly.

To make the bend, heat the piece at the bending point to yellow and quickly position it in the jig with a trial pin. Clamp the work to the jig and lock it in the vise so the top of the jig, where the bend is to be made, clears it. With the cross-peen, make the bend. There is no need to make a full right-angle bend. The leg can be held upright in tongs and the blows will start the curve but keep the angle. Bend both pieces in the same way.

To make the jig for the curves in the legs, first lay out a full-sized drawing on your surface plate. Bend a piece of flat steel, the same size as for the first jig, to fit the inside edge of the plan. Saw out a slot on one edge to receive the joint and clamp the work to the jig. For this bend the pin position can be disregarded, because both bends already made are equidistant from that point. Lock the jig in the vise, high enough so the work can clear it. Heat the piece, clamp it to the jig, and make the bend with round-nosed tongs, squeezing it up to the jig form.

Forge the guide pin from five-thirty-seconds-inch round rod. Thread and rivet it through one leg. Use a small oval punch to shape a hole in the other leg and pass the pin through it. The guide pin position on both legs should be the same distance from the pivot pin. Next rivet down the pivot pin and file it smooth.

The spring, which gives power to the jaws, is forged from mild steel in tapered section, from one-eighth-inch by one-half-inch stock. Spring steel is not needed here, because the point of spring bearing is so close to the axis that very little movement is given to the spring, which works on the same principle as does a wooden diving board, or a bent sapling.

Finally, after assembly, the pick-up disks can be filed to shape, and the tail and tamper given their final forms. When finished, thickness through the joint will be about three-eighths inch. This is ample for these tongs, which should be light in weight and rather delicate throughout.

If a black finish is desired instead of a bright one, there is no need to descale and polish. Instead, heat the piece over the fire and dip it in oil. Reheat and dip until the surface carbonizes and a satin black color appears. Wipe off all excess oil and rub with a cloth to polish.

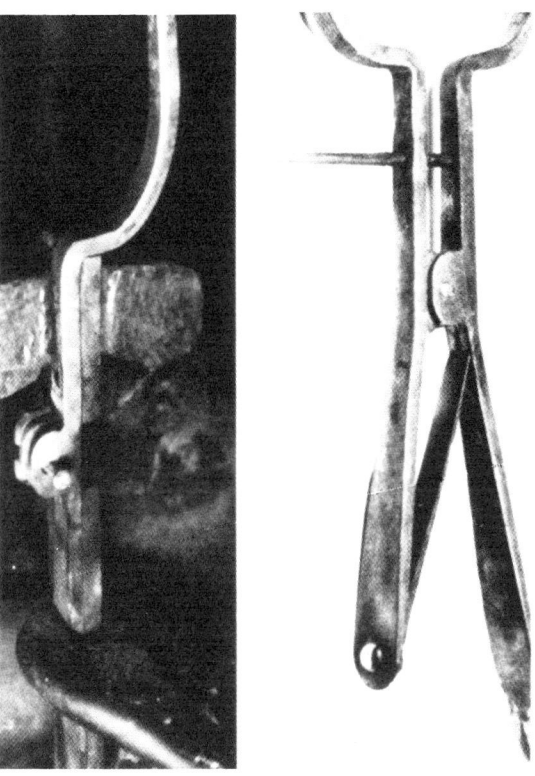

Left, bending the angle in the jig; right, finished joint and spring.

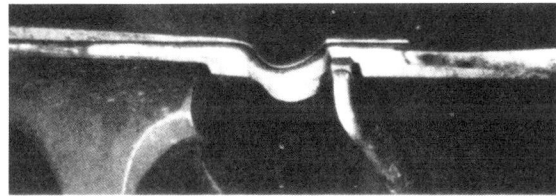

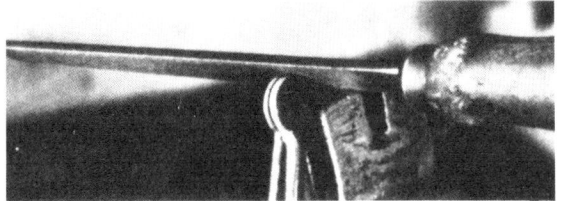

Top, bending the curve in the jig; bottom, filing the feet.

PIPE TONGS, ENGLISH

The original of this copy probably was made by an English whitesmith for export to the American colonies. The difference between it and the American form is apparent. Here, much more benchwork is involved, with some lathe turning, and a more exact joint required. Because of the length and design of the joint, no separate guide pin is required to hold the legs in line. The pivot pin extends into a turned stub that acts as a bowl scraper, and a turned disk makes the tamper. The tool is sixteen inches long and very light and delicate.

In most other respects it is made in much the same way as the American type. Therefore, attention is paid primarily to the formation of the joint. The stock used is half-inch-square mild steel. As in many cases where there are many differences in section in the finished forging, square stock is more satisfactory to use than rectangular, because it can be drawn either lengthwise or sidewise very rapidly without folding into shuts, which may mar the finish. Forge the legs and handles to roughly one-quarter inch thick, leaving stock for the joint. Reduce the joint stock to one-quarter inch thickness, three-quarter inch wide, and two and one-quarter inches long. Make

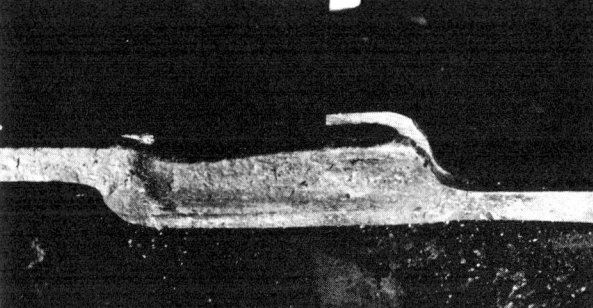
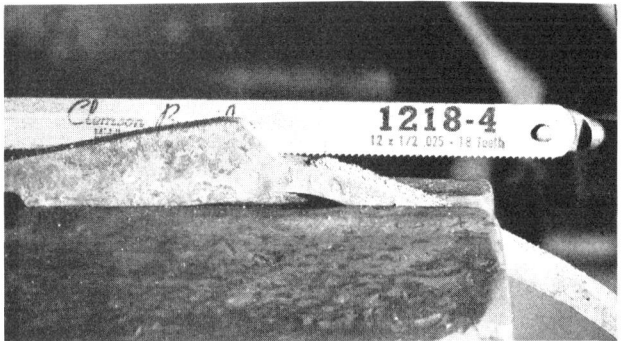

Top, the blank for the joint; bottom, sawing the female joint.

Top, cutting the slot; bottom, fitting it.

two pieces with the same-sized joints, but varying in the handle ends. Bend the handle of the female part for clearance, and saw a slot in its joint part down to the handle, but stopping short of the start of the leg. That end must remain solid, to give strength and hide the joint.

Heat the part, straighten the bend, and open the slot with a thin hot chisel, driving it down level with the handle. Heat again, and drive a steel strip, three-thirty-seconds inch thick, into the slot and close the sides against it, leaving the walls three-thirty-seconds inch thick. When finished, walls and joint leaf each will be one-sixteenth inch thick, from forging and filing.

Forge the male joint part as done with the American form, as closely as possible on the an-

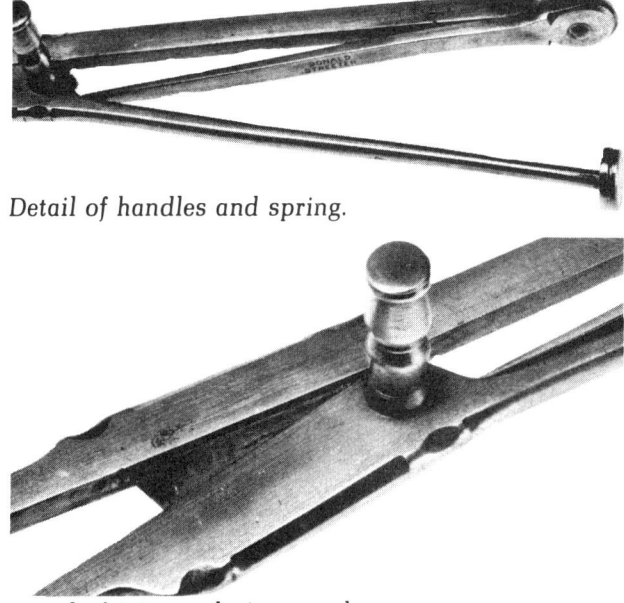

Detail of handles and spring.

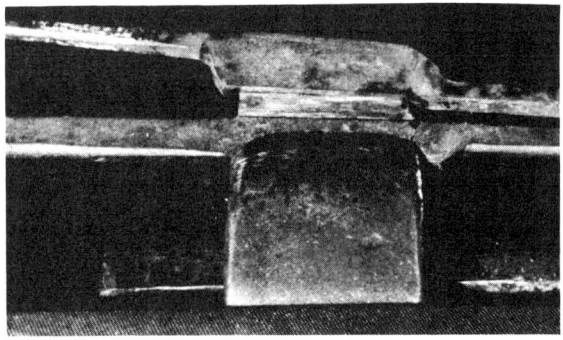

Detail of joint and pivot stud.

Top, use of vise in fitting male joint; bottom, filing it.

vil. At a yellow heat, drop the forged leaf into the vise and tighten the jaws. Strike the top edge, sharpening the corner. Then, with the part in the angle vise clamp, use a file with one sharp edge to file the leaf until it fits the slot.

The pivot is located very near the handle end of the joint, to assure that as the tongs open the leaf will remain in the slot and keep the legs aligned. The spring is of mild steel, tapered and bent so as to exert enough pressure to securely hold a hot coal. From the pivot point, the handles measure six inches.

Final filing should leave three-sixteenths-inch thickness throughout all flat parts, with the round tail tapering from flat at the joint to five-thirty-seconds inch round at the tamper disk.

STANDING BROILER

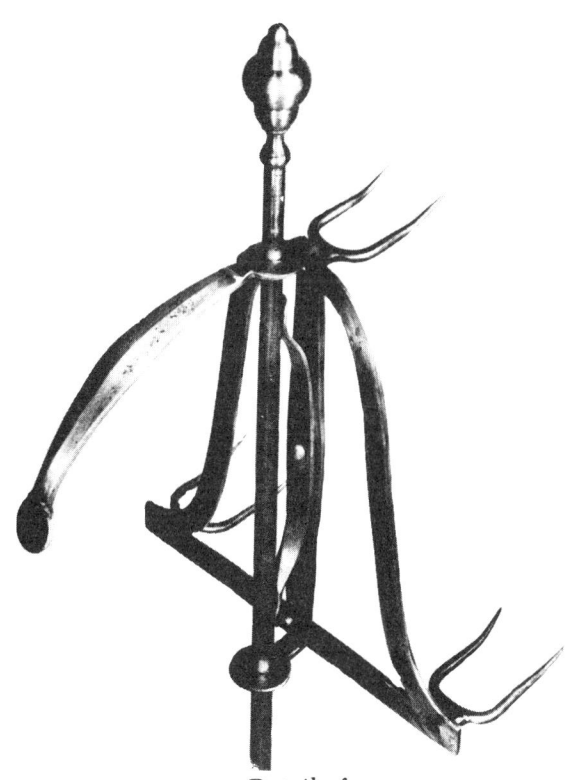

Detail of cage.

Kitchens in fine eighteenth-century houses often contained implements of this sort as fireside equipment. The broiler cage is adjustable in height and can be moved around the standard. It supports three forks on which bread can be toasted, or small birds broiled. Since no progress photographs were made during the fabrication of this broiler, these notes are offered as a guide to its forging.

Overall height is thirty-two inches. The center staff is seven-sixteenths-inch cold-finished steel round. Legs were forged from one-quarter-inch by one-inch hot-rolled steel, with the center ridge line formed in an anvil swage made for that purpose. The cage frame was done with three-sixteenths-inch by one-half-inch hot-rolled steel, in

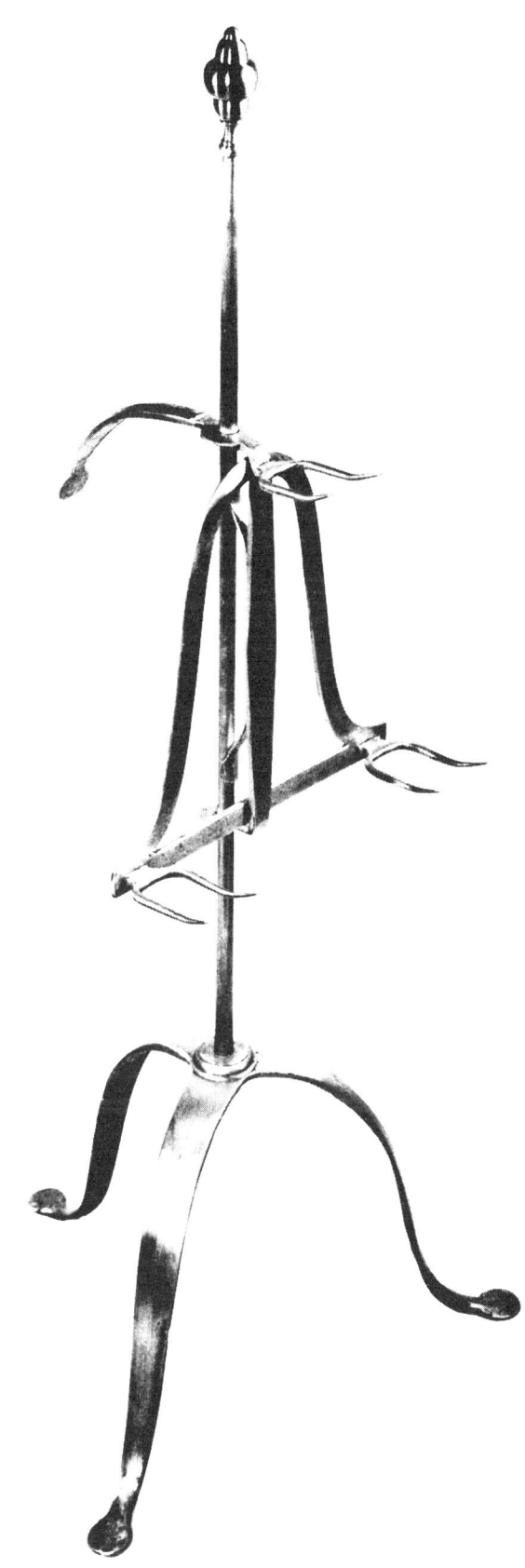

Standing broiler (Collection of the University Museum and Art Galleries, Southern Illinois University at Carbondale).

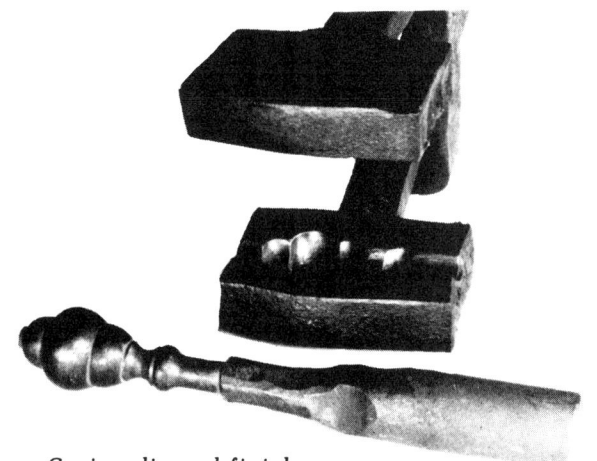

Spring die and finial.

two pieces, welded at the feet of the curve, then thinned to one-eighth inch by five-eighths inch. The arm that supports the cage and provides the handle was forged from three-eighths inch by one-inch wrought iron. The finial at the top of the shaft was made with one-inch round iron with a half-round collar welded around its widest point, then formed in a spring die, welded to the shaft, and finished on a lathe.

The tension spring, like others here described, is mild steel that has been tapered. Its ends were flared and cupped to fit the shaft. The forks were made as shown in the making of a flesh fork and riveted to the cage frame. All surfaces were draw-filed, polished bright, and waxed.

4 FIREPLACE IRONWORK

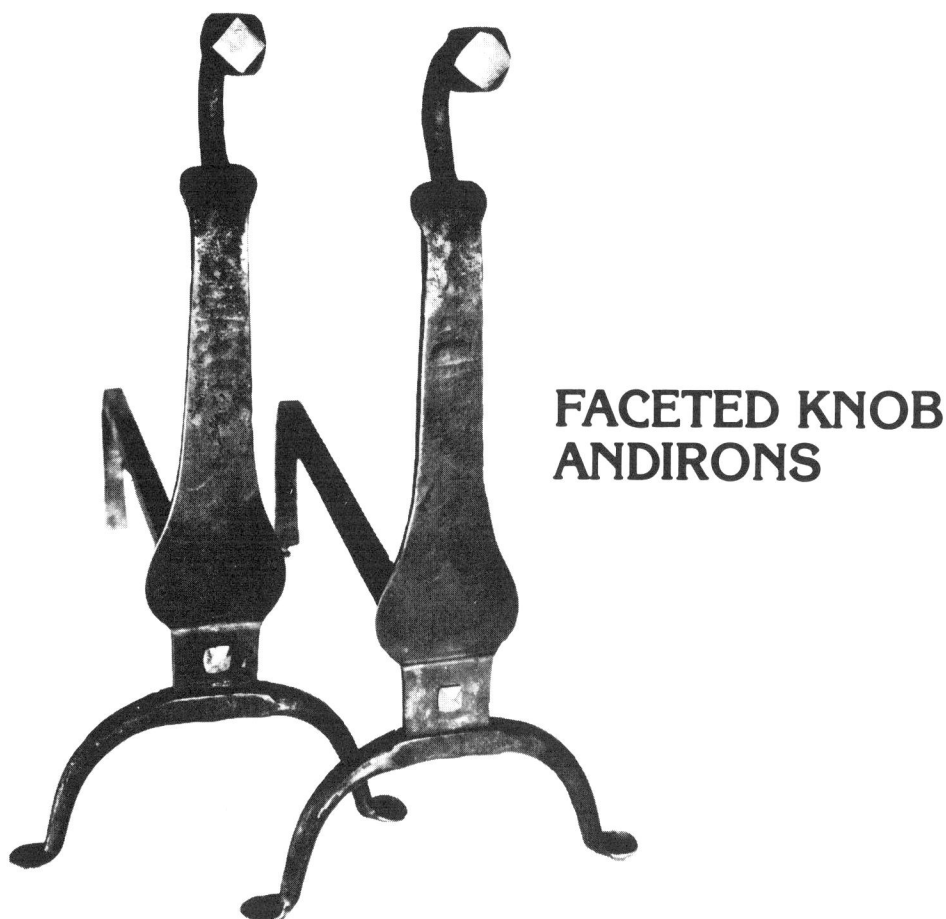

FACETED KNOB ANDIRONS

To make these andirons of traditional colonial form, choose flat bar stock of suitable size, in this case three-eighths inch by two and one-quarter inch for the uprights, and three-quarters inch square for the front and back legs. Since andirons must be a matching pair, start with two bars, so that as the forging progresses, each step can be done to match.

Starting at one end, forge the tenon that will pierce the front leg bar, finishing it as square as possible, by upsetting if needed, and by use of the set hammer. The tenon should be thinner than the upright, flat on what is to be the back, and with a

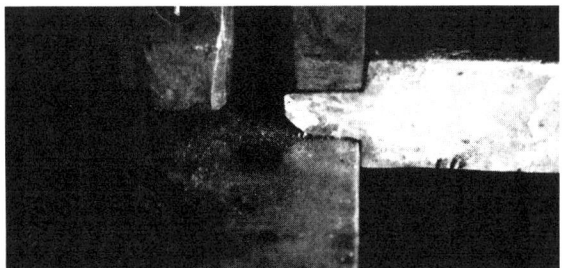

Top, forging the base tenon; bottom, starting the swelling.

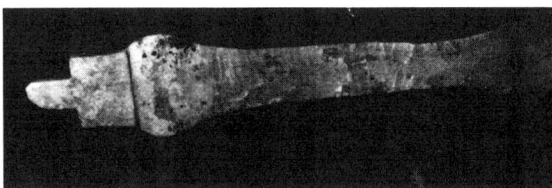

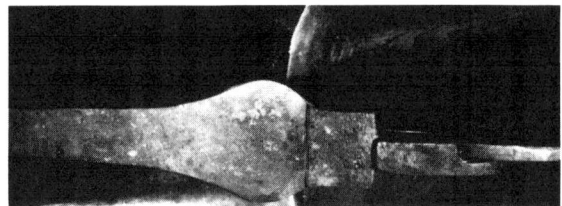

Top, drawing the shaft; bottom, refining the curves.

sharp shoulder at the upright's base. This is done not only to reduce the size of the mortise in the leg, but also to cover any irregularity in the mortise when assembled.

With the bar at yellow heat, bring it to the anvil and allow two inches of the main bar, behind the tenon, to project over a good square edge. Hold it firmly in position. Using a heavy hammer, strike good hard blows with the hammer face partly over the anvil edge, to drive the flat stock down and establish a shoulder line. Then, with the cross-peen, fuller the part on the anvil face sideways, thinning it at the edges and establishing a curve. Do this on the back side.

At another yellow heat, draw out the shaft above the curve so that it narrows in width in a graceful curve. As you approach the part where the round neck will be forged, keep the material as full as possible, to allow enough stock to make a neck of five-eighths-inch round section. Cut from the bar at a point that will allow this.

Flatten the shaft and refine the profile, using the horn of the anvil to dress the edges of the curves. Because of the taper of the horn, a great variety of curves can be accommodated there.

Forge the neck section to a full five-eighths inch round, and, with the work held at an angle across

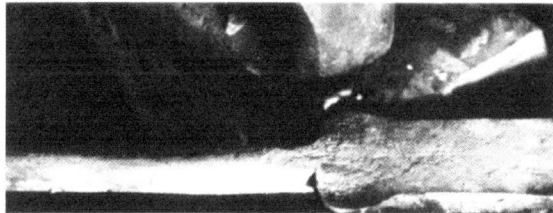

Top, forming the neck, bottom; forging the decorative ears.

an anvil corner, forge the decorative swellings where the neck joins the shaft in the same way as for the flesh fork (see page 32). Now lay both uprights alongside each other and check the match. All points of change in form must match, as well as overall length. If they differ, correct by drawing or upsetting. Cut off the round necks to equal lengths, sufficient to form the gooseneck of your design.

To form the faceted knobs, roll up two pieces of three-eighth-inch by one-inch stock into rings of equal size that fit snugly on the necks, leaving a gap of about one-eighth inch between the ends. This space is needed to allow the iron to move and join as the weld is made, first to the neck and then to itself. Without it the ring will move away from the shaft and spoil the weld.

Heat and flux the joint and weld all together in a round swage of proper size. Use light and rapid blows to avoid stretching. The object is to make a tight and neat weld without reducing size. If a helper is available, you can make an even neater joint by welding between top and bottom swages.

After the knobs are welded, square them on the anvil into cubes, aiming for equality of mass. Then hold the work at the near edge of the anvil, and rest it on one corner of the cube, with the shaft

Top, rolling the ring; bottom, welding to the neck.

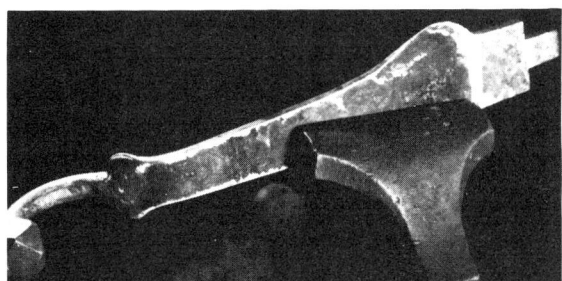

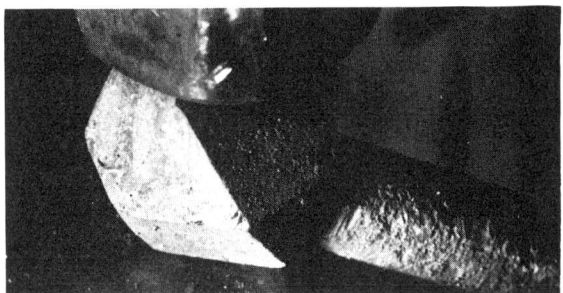

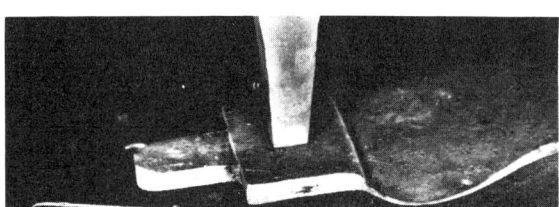

Top, shaft filed and bent; bottom, punching hole for back leg.

Top, squaring the knob; bottom, forging the facets.

pointing down. Using vertical flat blows parallel to the anvil face, forge the facets. Check all sides as the forging proceeds, and correct any irregularities before final shaping. Forging of the uprights is then complete, except for filing, bending, and piercing the base for the back leg.

File all edges to smooth profiles, and dress the knobs to final surfaces where necessary. Then bend the gooseneck, starting over the anvil edge and finishing over the horn, striking on the flat surfaces to avoid marring the neck.

Drill one-half-inch holes in the centers of the base section above the tenons, and square them with a one-half-inch square punch, clearing out the corners while hot.

Forge the front legs from three-quarter-inch square stock long enough to form the legs of your design. The legs shown here are thirteen inches. From center marks, draw each end to a diminishing round taper three-eighths inch in diameter, leaving a three-inch-square section at each center. Forge all to the same length. Forge penny feet at all ends, and bend to a little less than right angles.

At the center of each leg, in the square section, punch slots to fit the tenons. By filing as needed, fit them so that the tenon enters the slot and the shoulder rests squarely. It is important that this

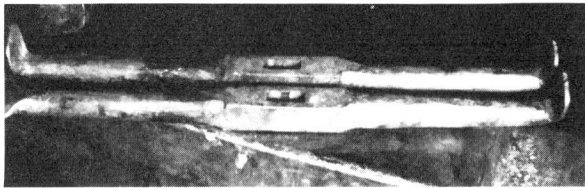

Top, front legs forged and punched; bottom, shaft tenon fitted.

Bending the front legs.

be done carefully for the shaft to stand upright when all legs are in place. Any error here will be hard to correct later. Trim the tenons to allow one-eighth inch to rivet down, or a little more if the joint is loose.

To assure that all leg curves are the same, make a bending form of three-quarter-inch square iron, fitted to the desired inside curve of the legs, on the end of a bar that projects from the vise far enough to be worked without cramping. The center of the bent leg should be at the end of the bar. Preset Vise-grip pliers to hold leg and form together. Take a good high heat and quickly position the leg on the form. Make the bend with a round top swage and hammer, to prevent hammer blows from marring the leg.

To join the shaft and front leg, heat both parts to red, and lock the shaft in the vise close to the tenon. With the cross-peen, spread the end out over the base of the leg. If only the tenon is heated, it may loosen as it cools. Both parts' shrinking together will assure a tight joint.

Forge a tenon on the end of a bar of three-quarter-inch square iron long enough for the back leg, trim it to size, and rivet it through the base of the shaft. The back leg is a simple right-angle bend, its end trimmed to make it stand upright.

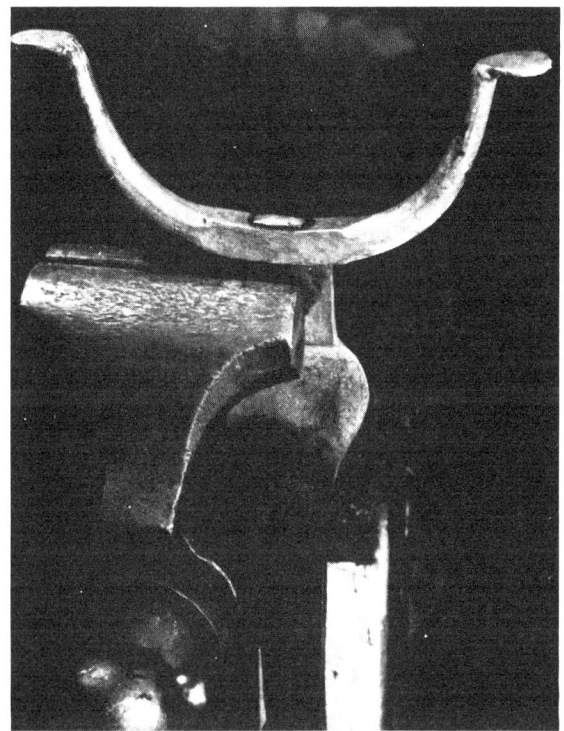

Assembling the andiron front.

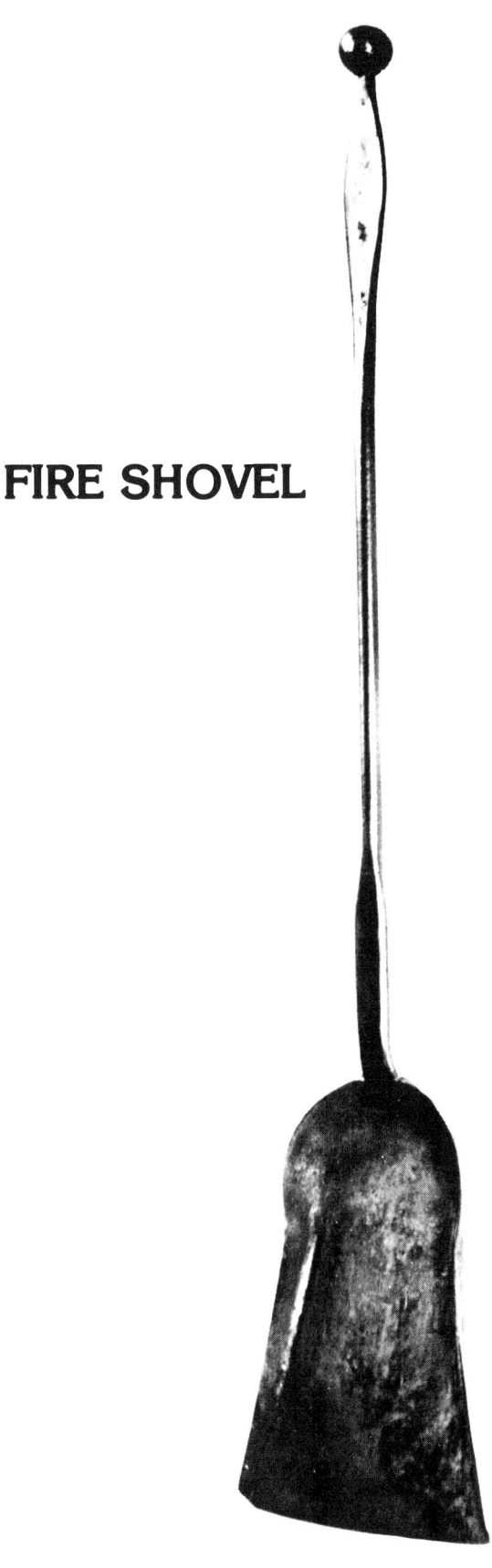

FIRE SHOVEL

This shovel with an integrally forged blade is made in much the same way as the kitchen ladle, differing mainly in shape and size. Although the easiest method is to rivet a separate blade of sheet steel to the handle, the method described here is the traditional way fine ones were forged.

For the handle, use half-inch round stock of the desired length. The one shown here is eighteen inches. Upset one end to about three-quarter inch round. Reduce it to three-eighths inch by three-quarter inch and scarf it for a lap weld.

Make the blade from a piece of flat stock, one-quarter inch by two inches by nine inches. Forge one end into a center neck, two inches long, three-eighths inch thick, and three-quarters inch wide, and scarf it. Weld both pieces together and dress down the section to five-sixteenths inch thick, blending into the round.

With a heavy cross-peen, or in the power hammer, starting in the center, spread the blank out into a blade to a final thickness of about one-sixteenth inch at the edges and somewhat thicker in the main body, and blending into the top where the handle starts. It will take several heats, so keep the edges a bit thick until the last heat, to avoid burning. Smooth the whole blade.

Make a cardboard pattern for the blade, and transfer it to the blank. You can scratch it with a scriber, but this is sometimes hard to see on the scale. Instead, try sticking masking tape on the blank and tracing around the pattern with a pencil. Cut along the lines and remove the tape.

The blade is formed most easily in a cast-iron mold made for that purpose. The mold may be found in some old swage blocks. Heat the blade to a red, and hammer it into the mold. Old hammers with spoiled edges can be reground to form raising hammers to do this sort of work, so that they follow the curves without denting the piece. The cross-peen is used to raise the sides, whose corners can be sharpened on the edges of the anvil, or in the vise. After the blade is shaped, file to final form.

Top, handle and blade blanks; bottom, blade and handle welded.

Blade roughly forged.

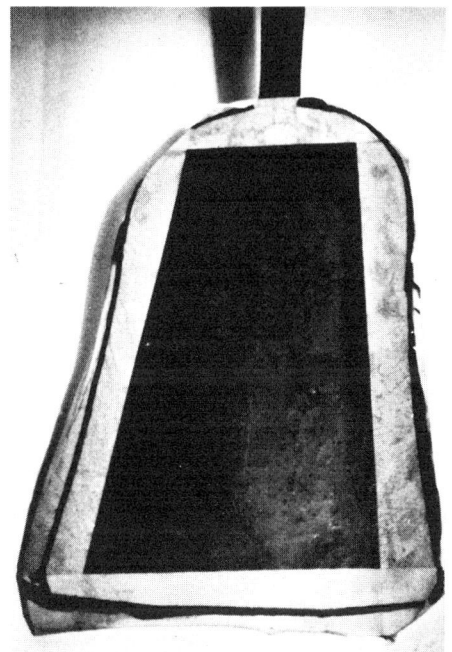

Blade pattern traced on blank.

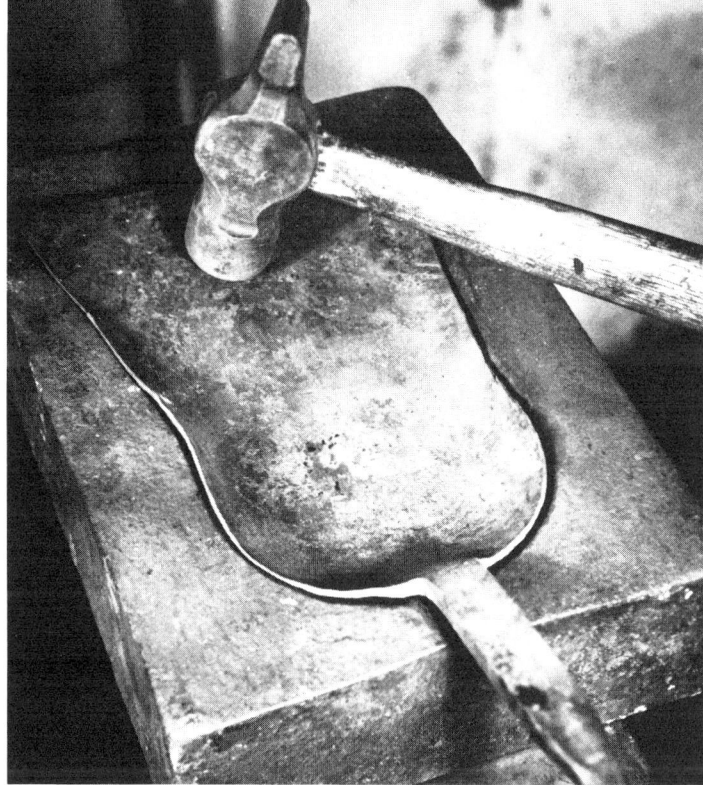

Raising the blade.

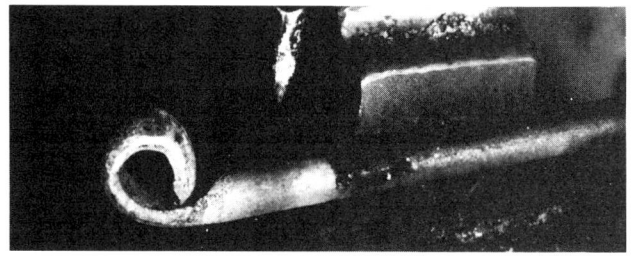

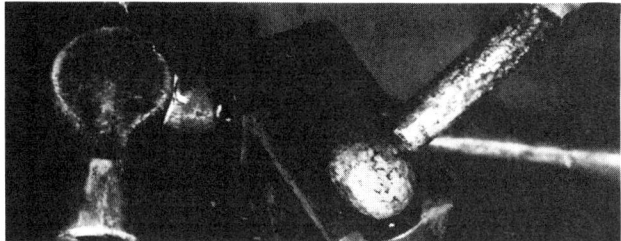

Top, the knob ring; bottom, knob welded to shaft.

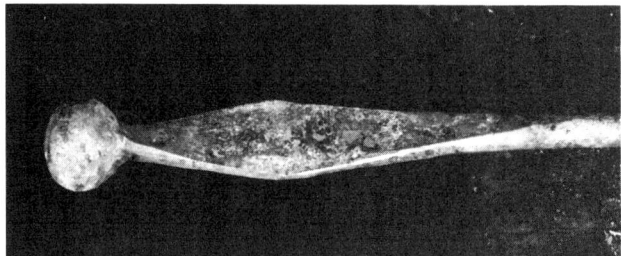

Handle detail.

The handle is a simple round knob with a swelling below it for a hand grasp. Make the knob the same way the andiron knob was formed, by welding a collar to the round and shaping it. In this case, since the knob is to be round instead of a faceted cube, make the collar from five-eighth-inch round iron, flattened in a three-quarter-inch round swage. Cut it off and weld it to the round in the swage, finishing with the hammer. Grind or file to remove all flats.

Below the knob, forge the shaft out into a swelling, thick at the center, and tapering to rounded edges. File to shape, and bend the shovel at the throat to an angle convenient for use. Heat and blacken with oil.

FIRE TONGS

Using three-quarter-inch square iron, draw out one end to slightly under one-half inch thick by six inches long, tapering at the end to five-eighths inch wide. This will be a little fuller than your finished size. Leave a sharp shoulder where the reduction starts.

Rest the forging on a soft-steel cutting plate. Using a thin, sharp, hot chisel at a slight angle from the shoulder, cut through. Turn the bar over and cut through from that side, following the same angle, which is necessary to provide clearance for movement of the joint. Drive a punch of proper size through and square the slot.

With another bar of the same size, forge a flat section to match the first, but leave an inch of square bar at the end. Forge this into a flat tongue at right angles to the flat and centered with it. Line up the flat side of the bar by placing the tongue in the vise and striking the top edge, which will give sharp corners and make the outside face even. See that the tongue is flat and wide enough to fill the slot.

Check for fit of the joint. If too tight, file one piece or the other. If too loose, upset the tongue or forge a new end. This is the heart of the tongs, and now is the last chance to correct any errors. Fit need not be final, but at least assure yourself that the pieces can be filed to a neat fit later.

Left, cutting the slot; right, squaring it.

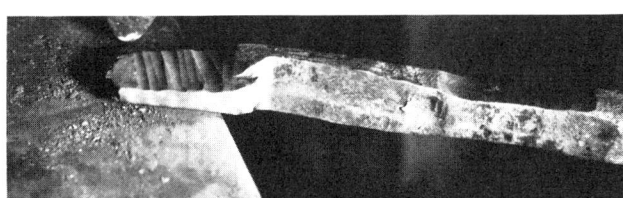
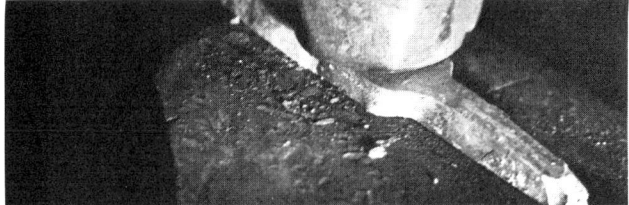

Top, forging the tongue; bottom, squaring the joint.

In order to produce a soft inside corner that will not form a hot shut when upsetting, heat a piece of three-sixteenth-inch band stock, lock it in the vise, and bend it around the jaw to hold it in place. This is better than altering the jaw edge. Bend the flat of the female part over the band, using the bottom of the vise jaw as a gauge at the shoulder. Remove the vise strap and lock the part in place with the start of the bend curve resting on the jaw. At a yellow heat, with the cross-peen, draw some of the extra thickness of the flat part back toward the corner, upsetting at the same time. Remove the part from the vise and finish sharpening the corner by upsetting at the anvil. Chill any part that may bend, in order to concentrate the blows in the proper place.

Mark the point of the second bend at one and one-half inches from the end, and record it so the other piece can be bent the same. Fit the vise strap in place again and make the bend the same way as

Left, making the first bend; right, upsetting the corner.

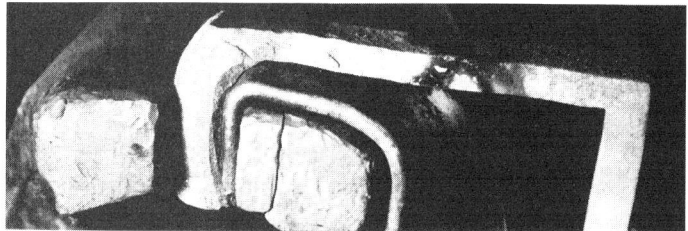

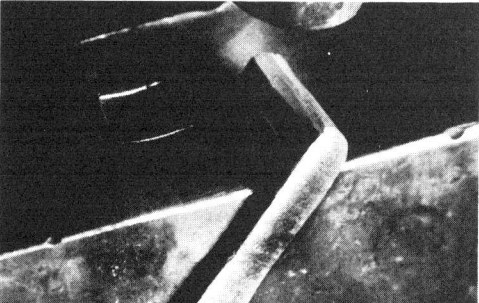

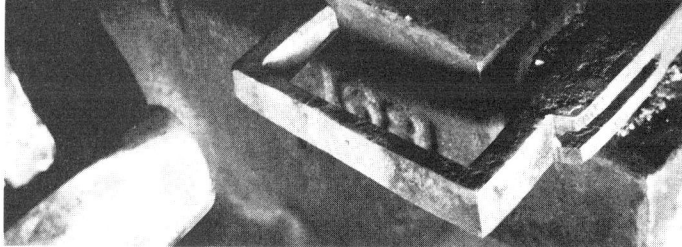

Top, making the second bend; bottom, upsetting the corner.

Top, rounding the nub; bottom, locating the pivot.

Top, matching the corners; bottom, rough forging fitted.

the first. Upset the corner as before. This can be done by holding the work so that the short nub rests against the far side of the anvil while working on the corner. The nub now must be forged into round section, as full as possible, to assure enough stock for welding to half-inch round. Slip the piece under the heel of the anvil and rest it on the top face in order to work most handily.

Now that both bends are completed in the female part, the joint should be fitted before doing the male part, since, in order to line up, all bends should be the same distance from the pivot point. Lay out diagonal lines from the corners of the parallelogram formed by the edges of the slot, and drill a five-thirty-second-inch hole where they intersect, for an assembly pin, smaller than the finish pin to allow for correction.

With the vise strap in place, and the joint pinned together, make the first bend in the male part. Remove the trial pin and upset the corner. Replace the pin and, with the work in the vise, line up this corner with the female corner.

Then, from your recorded distance, mark and

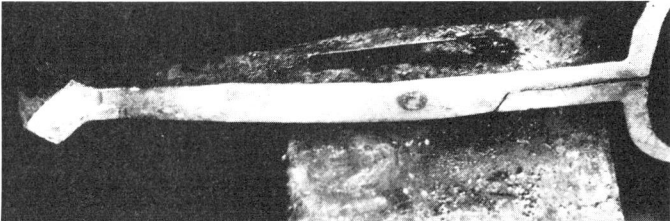

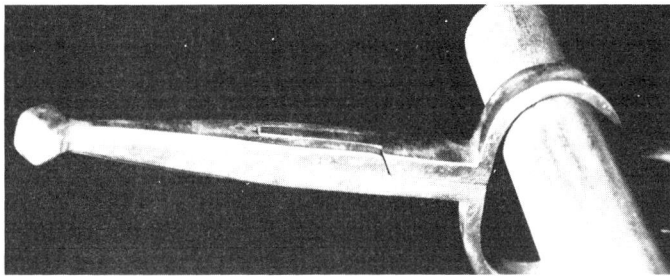

Top, the handle; bottom, truing the eye.

make the second bend, upsetting and rounding the nub in the same way as the female part. Check all lengths, widths, and sections for equality, and correct where needed. Allowing enough bar stock for the handle, cut off the female part. The work will be easier to hold from now on if not part of a long bar.

Bend the eye, not over the horn, where twists may develop, but over a pipe or mandrel of cylindrical form, to keep a flat ribbon type of curve.

Upset and scarf the round nubs after removing the assembly pin. Scarf two pieces of half-inch round stock for the legs, of length suitable for your design, and weld them to the nubs. Cut them to equal lengths and forge small disks at each end, tapering the legs behind them. With the joint clamped shut and with the legs clamped together at the ends, correct any imbalance in the curves, and center the tips in line with the handle part.

Forge the handle finial by forging a neck and a faceted knob at the end, or a round one, to suit your choice.

FIRE FORK

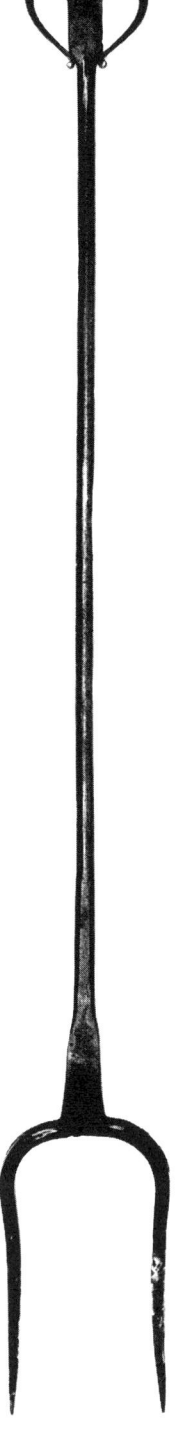

Making this fork is more an exercise in welding than forging, since there are no great changes in form, but rather a union of round and flat stock. Sizes used are one-half-inch round for the handle shaft, three-eighths inch by one inch for the fork end, and one-quarter inch by three-quarter inch for the handle grip.

To make the tines, heat a bar of three-eighths inch by one inch. Over a narrow fuller at four and one-half inches from the end, forge two notches halfway through, leaving an inch of full stock between them for a welding boss. Cut from the bar at a point that will give equal lengths for the tines, and draw each down to seven-sixteenths inch square. Trim them to desired lengths and point them. Scarf the boss for a T weld. Sometimes it is helpful in this type of weld to cut small notches on the scarf on the corner of the hardy. This helps to avoid slipping, and the fine edges raised by the cut will melt first in the heat in the same way that iron filings do in a commercial flux.

Using a five-inch bar of the same stock, scarf one end for welding to the tines' boss. Forge the other end to an octagonal, tapering into the flat, and scarf it for welding to round stock. This will form a transition section from the tines to the handle and add strength, balance, and design. Weld it to half-inch round of any desired length and dress it so the octagonal will blend into the round.

Bow the tines, to help keep them flat for the weld and out of the way of the hammer. Weld handle and tines together and shape the fork end.

At the handle end of the round, draw two inches to about one-quarter inch by seven-eighths inch, upset, and scarf for welding. Draw a piece of one-quarter-inch by three-quarter-inch flat to form a T weld, reducing each end to thin tapers about four inches long, with a boss in the center. Make the weld and reduce the thickness to three-sixteenths inch. File so that all curves balance and ends are equal. Form small scrolls at each end and bend them so that the scrolls nest in the curve at the junction of flat and round.

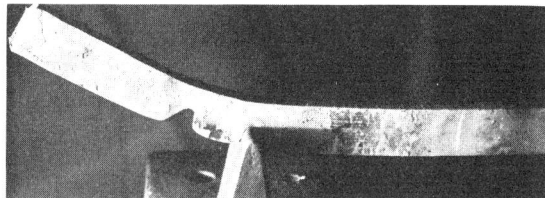

Top, fullering the leg blank; bottom, drawn and scarfed.

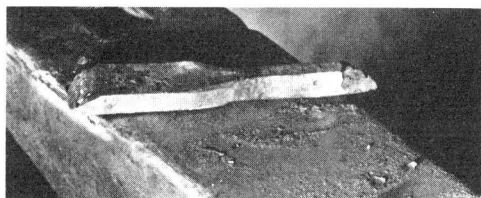

Top, transition piece; bottom, handle end.

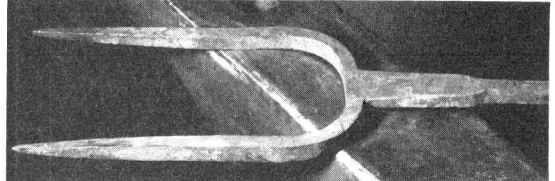

Top, tines ready to weld; bottom, weld completed.

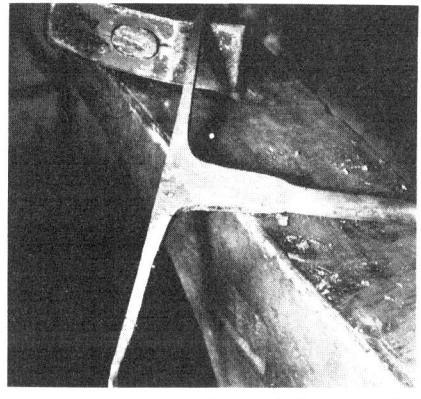

Top, grasp piece forged; bottom, the T weld.

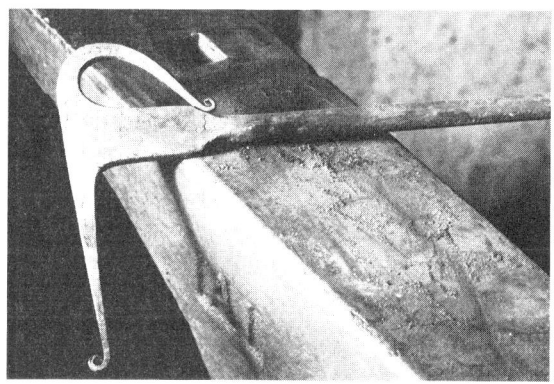

Bending the grasp.

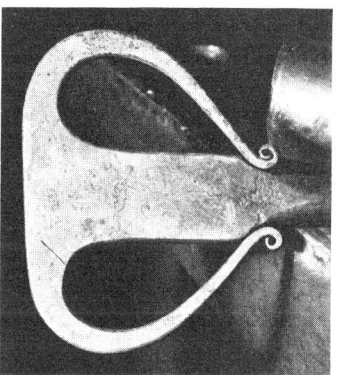

Handle detail.

FIREPLACE CRANE

In colonial cooking fireplaces a crane was essential to provide a movable arm from which to hang pots and spits. Upper and lower ends of the upright shaft rotated in holes in anchors set into the bricks. Since the upper round neck is longer than the bottom one, the crane could be removed from its anchors when necessary, or when setting the anchors. They were made to fit their places, and usually ran well past the center of the fire, rotating out over the hearth for loading or unloading.

Having determined the desired size, draw out the top arm from a rectangular bar of suitable size, tapering in width from full at the post to slender at the upturned end.

Forge the upright from square stock. Because the crane shown here is small, one-inch size was used. Work the end down to about five-eighths inch round, finishing in the round swages, allowing three inches of round section. Use a bolster, or steel block with a suitable hole. Heat the bar yellow and ram it down against the block to square up the corners. Forge the other end in the same way, but leave only an inch of round, and upset in the bolster to increase the bearing surface.

For decorative purposes, forge the corners of the shaft down to modified octagonal section, leaving space at top and bottom in the original size. Forge a tenon on the thick end of the top bar to pierce the upright. Make a steel punch the size of the tenon and punch a slot through the upper square part and fit mortise and tenon by filing or forging. Often the fit can be made by driving the cold tenon through the hot slot. Trim the tenon to allow one-eighth inch for riveting down in assembly.

Forge a diagonal brace to any suitable form— here a simple twisted square bar which is tapered

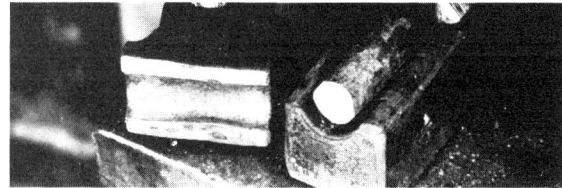

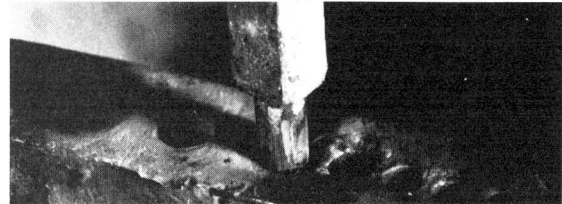

Top, forming round section; bottom, upsetting shoulders.

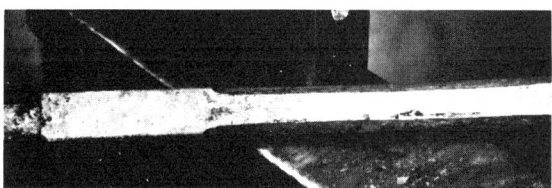

Top, chamfered corners; bottom, the tenon of the top bar.

Mortise-and-tenon joint fitted.

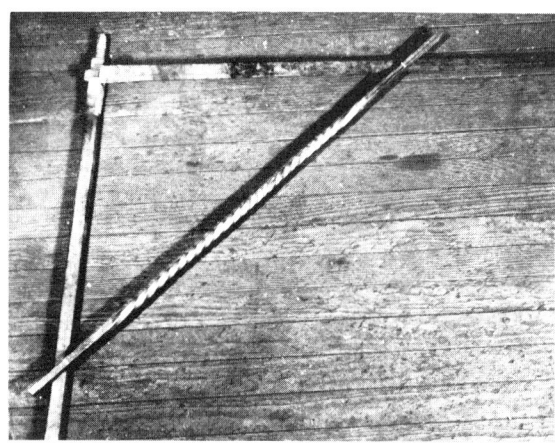

Layout.

at each end—but no wider at the top than the thickness of the top bar. Lay out all pieces on the floor or other flat surface. Square the top corner, and mark the points where bends must be made in the brace.

Prepare the top arm and brace for welding by bending the tip of the brace so only the surface that is to be welded touches, and wire them in position. Bring both to a welding heat and weld only the center of the curve, leaving unjoined the parts for bend and scroll.

With the weld held in the vise, carefully open the brace to its proper angle, the bottom bend having been made before the weld. When trial assembly proves a proper fit, bend the tip of the brace into its scroll.

Heat both mortise and tenon, and rivet together. Drill and rivet the bottom of the brace to final form.

Top, preparing the brace weld; bottom, weld made.

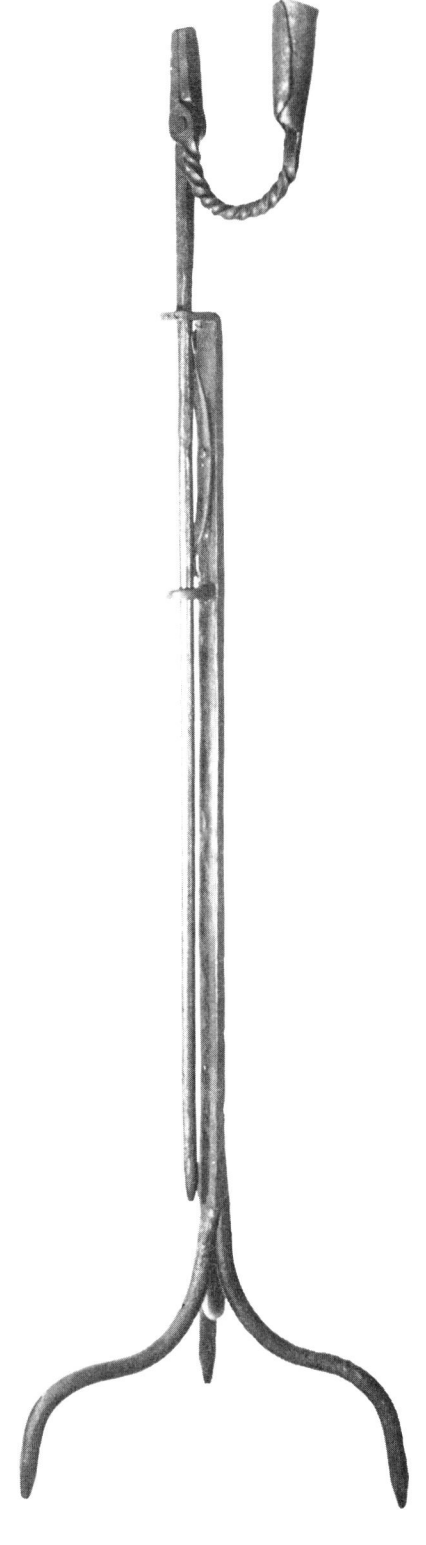

RUSH LIGHT
FLOOR STAND

Unlike the box joint rush light shown on page 42, this one is fairly primitive in form. It was finished with the hammer, and has feet that indicate its use at the hearth or other rough floor. Its height is adjustable, and it can be held in any side position by the spring, fastened to the upright and bearing upon the sliding leg. It stands twenty-eight inches below the tongs, and can be extended another twenty inches. Since projection from the staff is slight, it is stable, a governing factor in safety design of open-flame lights.

Following the shop drawings (page 75) for this piece, start with the legs of the stand. Using a bar of half-inch round, at nine and one-half inches from the end, heat it, and on a sharp hardy, cut it almost through. Bend it back against the bar, and where its end lies, cut the bar again, at 90° to the first cut. Bend it back so it lies astride the center of the other two, and the ends meet. They are now in welding position, with the rest of the bar available as a working handle. Heat the end and weld all together, with as short a lap as possible, to avoid reducing the round stock back too far. Scarf for a lap weld to flat stock.

Using a bar of one-quarter-inch by one-inch material, reduce it in width to seven-eighths inch. Upset and scarf the end and cut off at nineteen inches. Weld it to the welded rounds and forge down to a neat transition. Trim off and cut apart the joined round legs. Before bending the legs, forge and fit the top of the shaft. It will be easier to handle in the forge this way.

With a tapered round punch, hot punch a one-quarter-inch hole in the center of the flat, three-quarter inch from the end. With the punch in place over the jaws of the vise, expand the hole to allow a three-eighths-inch round bar to move

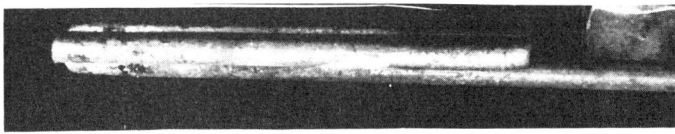

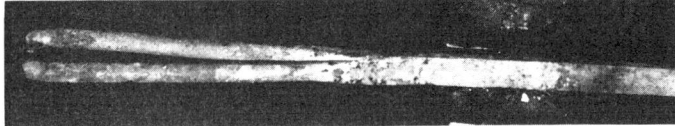

Top, legs bent for welding; bottom, legs welded to shaft.

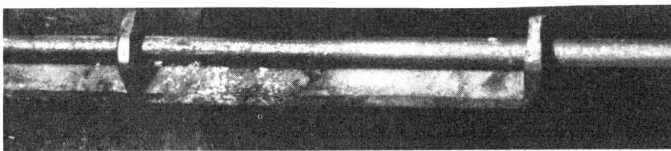

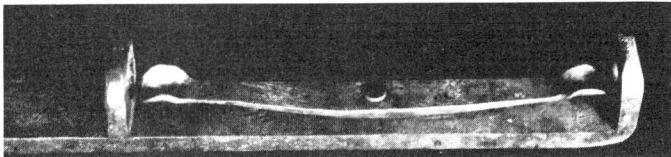

Top, sliding leg detail; bottom, spring.

freely in it, at the same time swelling the bar around the hole for strength. Round the end.

With another piece of bar of similar size, do the same thing. Bend the top of the shaft at a right angle, three-eighths inch below the punched hole. Cut off the second punched part to allow the holes to line up and leave enough stock to form a tenon one-quarter inch square by three-eighths inch long. Saw out the tenon and punch a square hole in the shaft, five and three-quarters inches down from the inside of the bend. Fit together. When a three-eighths-inch round bar can be passed through both holes parallel to the shaft, rivet in place.

Forge the spring from spring steel, or mild steel if necessary, thinning the ends and flaring them to form cups to bear upon the sliding leg. Bend to shape, adjust tension, and rivet in place.

Use of the tripod template.

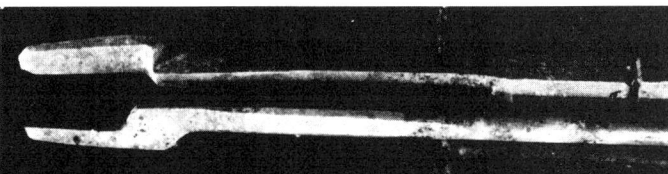

Top, jaws forged; bottom, candle cup blank forged.

To bend the legs of this light stand or any form with a tripod base, it is helpful to have a template to determine when angles are right. To make a template, bend pieces of strap iron of light weight and weld them together so that the center line of each leg forms an angle of 120°. Make the first leg bend after separating the legs to approximate angle, and try it on the template. Correct any inequalities before making the second, or bottom bend, over the anvil horn.

After this bend, point the end of each leg bluntly round, and again check each leg on the template. Chalk marks at an equal distance from the center of the template will gauge the correctness of the bends as the center of the staff stands over the center of the template. By sighting along some constant vertical edge such as a door or window frame, the plumb can be determined. If the vertical edge is not itself plumb, try this. Turn the piece one-third at each sighting. If the angle seen between the shaft and edge is the same at each turn, the work will stand plumb on a level surface. Usually one leg is shorter or longer than the others, and can be corrected quickly.

In essence, the rush light itself is simply a pair

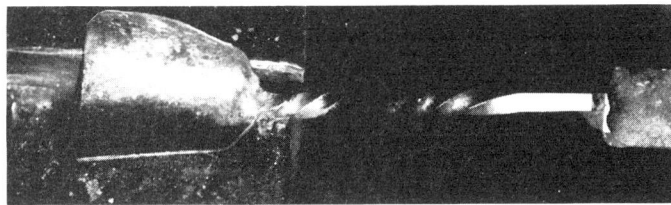

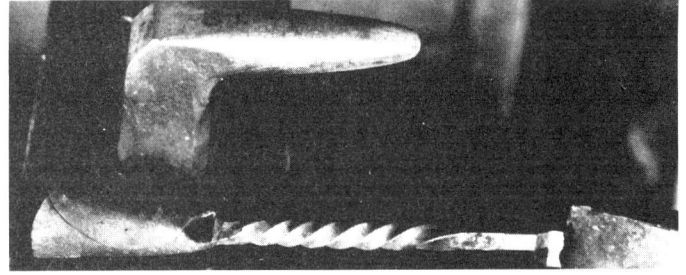

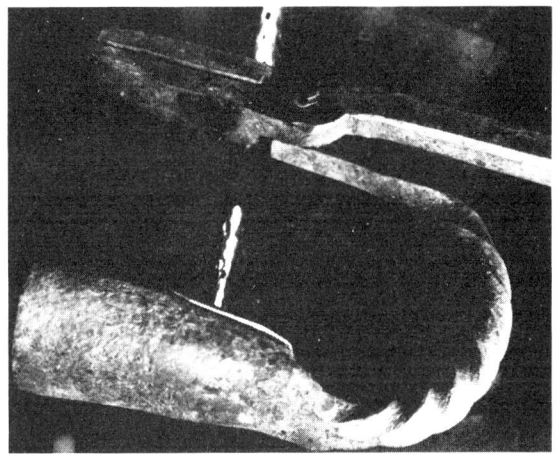

Top, starting the cup; bottom, cup formed and twist made.   *Detail of cup and tongs.*

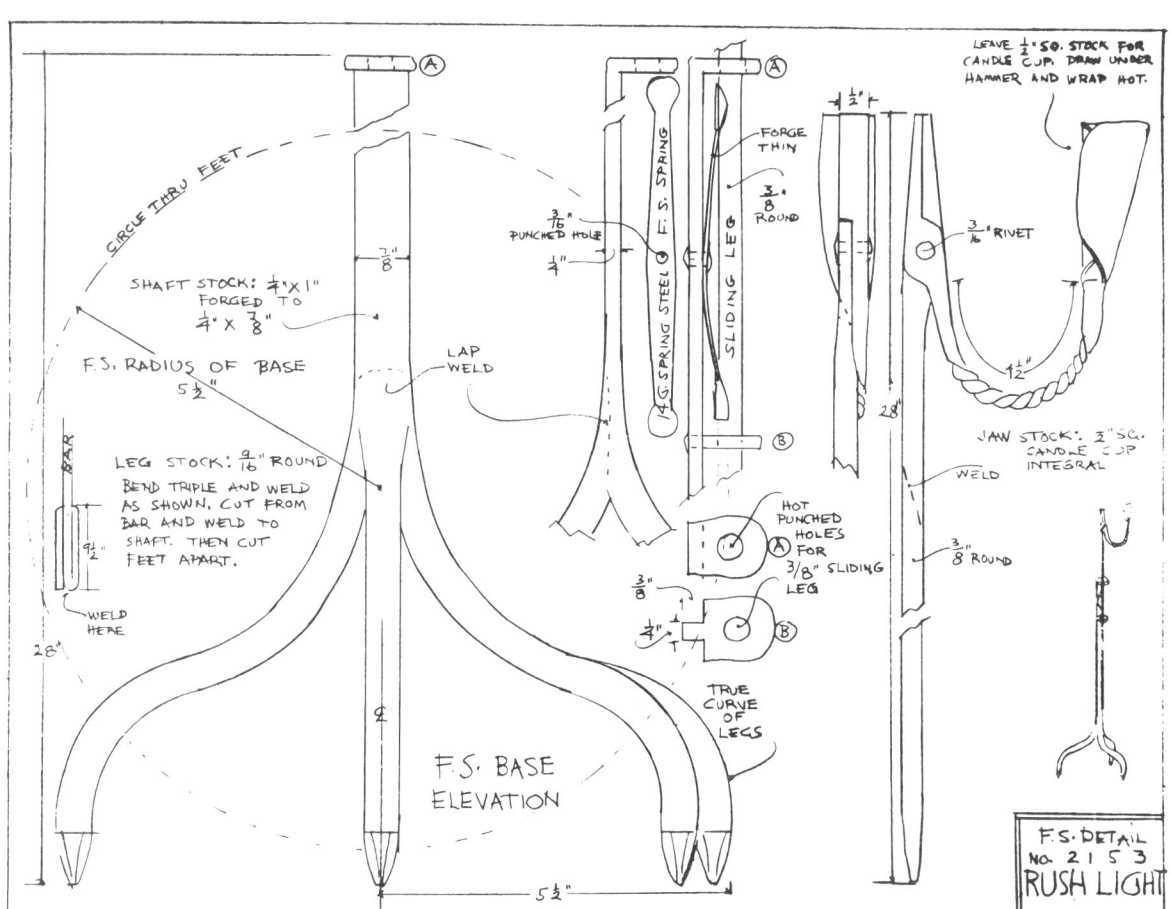

Shop drawing for the rush light stand.

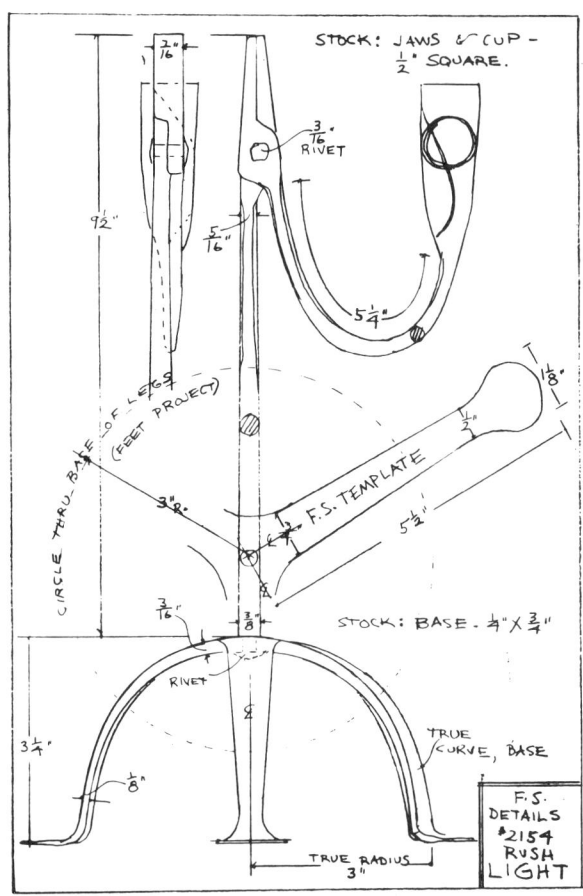

Shop drawing for a table rush light stand.

of light blacksmith's tongs, with a candle cup added as a counterweight on one rein. With half-inch square steel or iron, forge one jaw and weld it to a length of three-eighth-inch round stock long enough to measure twenty-eight inches overall. Forge the other jaw so as to leave a four-and-one-half-inch section one-quarter inch square between the base of the jaw and a two-inch-long square section of original stock for the cup. Spread the square nub out flat and thin to at least three inches, and smooth the surface. Fit the jaws for a rivet. Heat the slender square section, and give it two full twists.

Trim the top edge of the cup blank, then heat it. Form the cup by starting with the cross-peen, between anvil edge and table, and finishing on a beak fitted into the hardy hole. Rivet the joint and dress it, then bend the curve in the twist so the cup stands straight.

5 HARDWARE

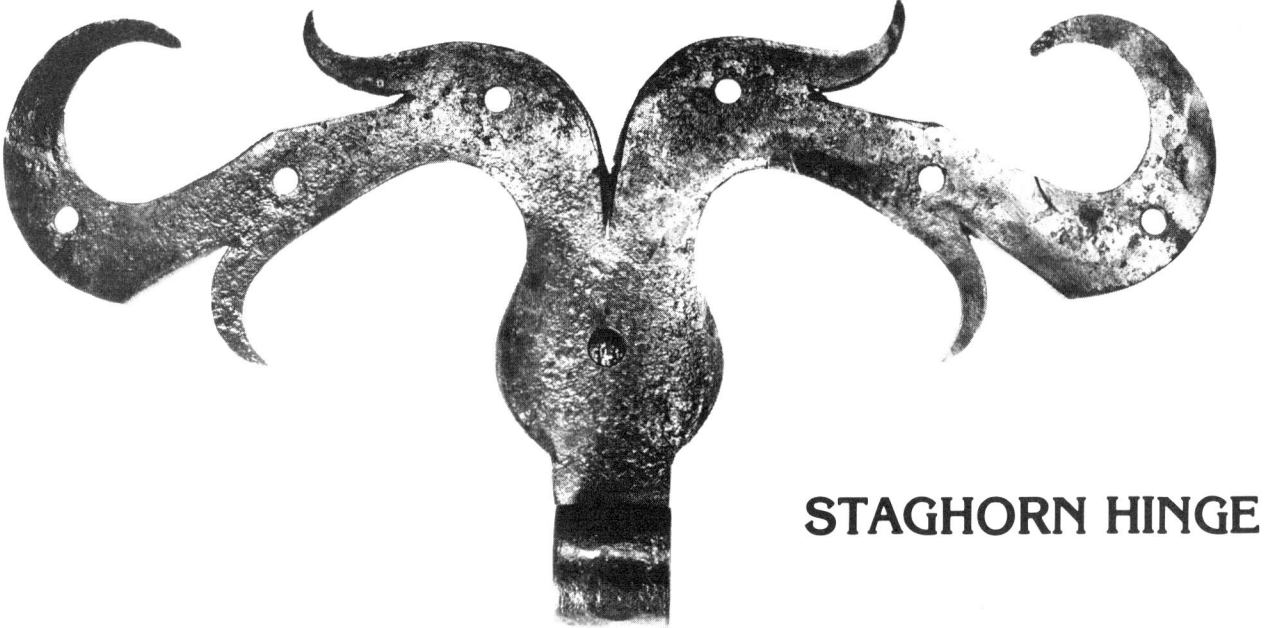

STAGHORN HINGE

To forge this hinge, take a bar of flat stock—in this case three-sixteenths inch by one and one-half inches—of any suitable dimensions, and bring its end to a yellow heat for about six inches. Prepare a cutting pad of soft steel about one-eighth inch thick, and wide enough for the purpose, by bending two sides down to form a channel that will fit over the anvil face. Place the hot iron upon it. With the hot cutter, split the iron down the center as far as need be for your hinge—in this case four and one-half inches. Use a thin sharp cutter, to cut fast and not form too wide a bevel at the cut. If you have a shear that will cut the metal hot or cold, use it. In any case, see that the split is centered so that both sides have the same volume.

At another heat, bend one leg back over the flat of the bar and forge the flat end to a point, thinning it in both directions but not reducing the

Splitting the end.

Top, one end bent and one forged; bottom, both ends forged.

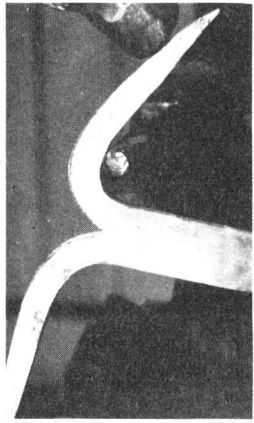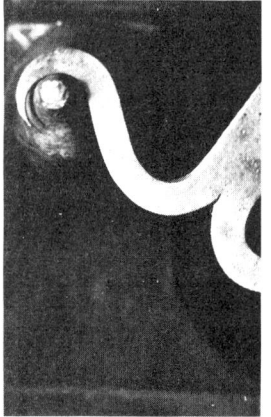

Left, starting the curves; right, curves completed.

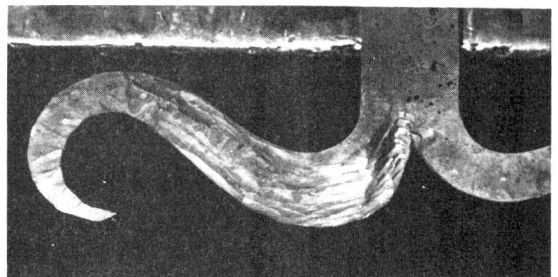

Fullering with the cross-peen.

weight of material in the body of the leg. Record its length, bend it out of the way, and forge the other leg to the same size. Flatten them both. At another heat, spread the two legs apart, either on the hardy or in any other practical way, enough so you can hit them with the hammer. While the heat holds, quickly bend one and then the other over the horn to the proper curve. Do not strike the hot iron against the horn, which will produce a flat, but deliver the blows past the horn so the metal is pulled or driven around it. Bending is the object, not forging. Check for balance by holding the work upright with the curves resting on the anvil. By turning the work from side to side, any differences in the legs can be seen and corrected.

Heat each end in turn, and bend it over the horn to its curve, seeing that both S curves visually match. The main structure of the staghorn now is made. However, the finished hinge is to be much thinner at the horns that the present weight would indicate. There is a reason for not thinning the horns first, and that is the difficulty thin iron presents when trying to bend it edgewise. Then it is apt to curl instead of bend. It is faster and better to bend it when thick, then thin it where desired.

This is done with the cross-peen, a lighter one than was used with the forging and bending. With good hammer control the hot iron can be drawn in any direction to take whatever form your design requires. It will be found that this method is surprisingly easy, and far faster than roughly forging a blank and cutting it out with chisels or a nibbler.

With the iron at an orange heat, to avoid burning thin edges, flatten and smooth the work and refine the curves. With the iron again on the cutting pad, use the hot chisel and cut the slits that will form the prongs to make the staghorn form. Make the cuts from the same side used to cut the split, so that all bevels made by the chisel will be on the hinge's face. This will save filing them later.

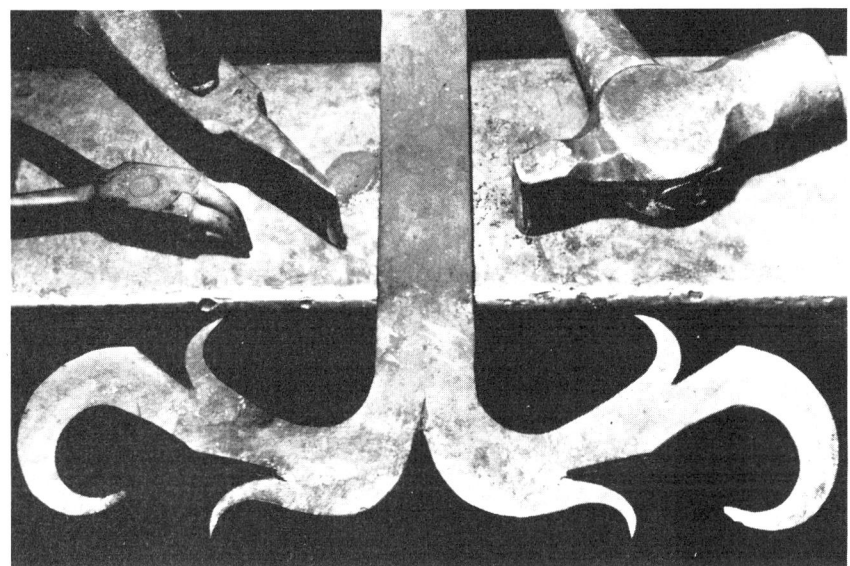

Cutting and bending the points.

Heat again and bend the scrolls, using whatever tools best suit your purpose. The hot chisel can be used to pry them open, and round-nosed pliers, here bent at a right angle for this sort of work, will help, as will a light hammer.

So far all forging has been done at the end of the bar. Now it must be cut off and held in tongs. Forge down a tail section to form the strap and eye. Make it long enough to fit the place where the hinge will hang. Reduce the width and increase the thickness for strength. Forge it very thin at the end, so it will roll up neatly in the eye.

Now turn the hinge face down on the anvil. With the cross-peen, fuller out the iron at the shoulder left when forging the tail so that it spreads out into a curve, taking care not to thin the strap part in its center. Prevent thin parts from burning in the fire by water cooling. At another heat, refine the curves and smooth the taper left by the fullering so that all lines flow gracefully. This is most easily done on the horn, where soft, glancing blows can safely forge the work down to a thin edge.

The next step is to roll in the eye. A hinge eye should resemble a cylinder. One must overcome

Fullering the cusp.

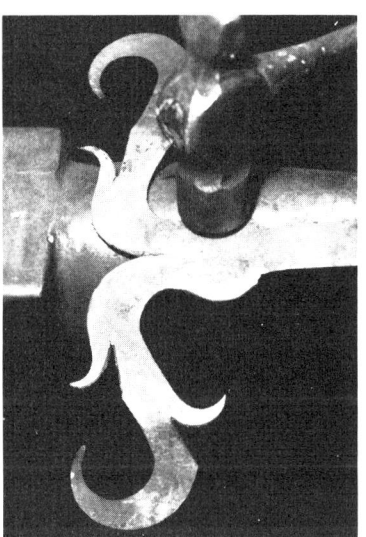

Finishing the cusp on the horn.

Curving the eye blank.

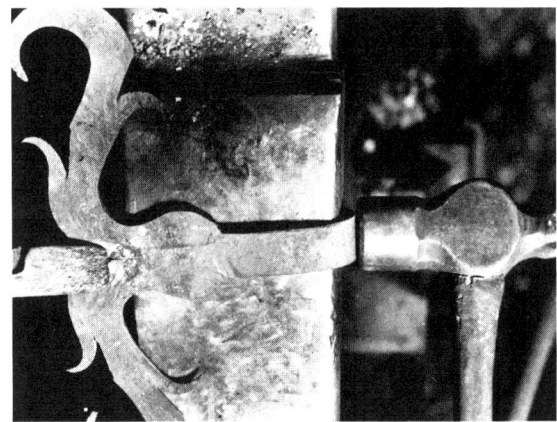

Starting the eye roll.

the tendency of flat iron to curl out of flat when bent into a curve. To do this the tail piece for the eye is first cupped lengthwise in the opposite direction. That is, a concave section is produced on the side that will be the inside wall of the eye, on the face side of the hinge. Then whatever stress causes the iron to curl will now cause it to straighten. Sometimes what appears to be this sort of outside curve on old hinges of this type is actually a fuller groove made in the tail before rolling up, to conserve weight and add decorative quality. The inside of the eye, however, is usually a cylinder.

The eye is started as for any freehand scroll, over a soft far edge of the anvil. Hold it so the tip projects past the edge. Using a series of light blows, with the hammer at an angle, glance them off the work, rolling the eye a little at a time. Complete the roll on the anvil top, coaxing the yellow iron into a tight roll the size the pin will require, with the tip of the tail snug against the wall of the eye. It is often easier to get a true round eye of proper size by rolling it a little tight and driving a mandrel of final size through the hot roll. It is crucial that the start of the roll be right, since it is hard to correct an error once the eye is done.

HINGE PINTLES

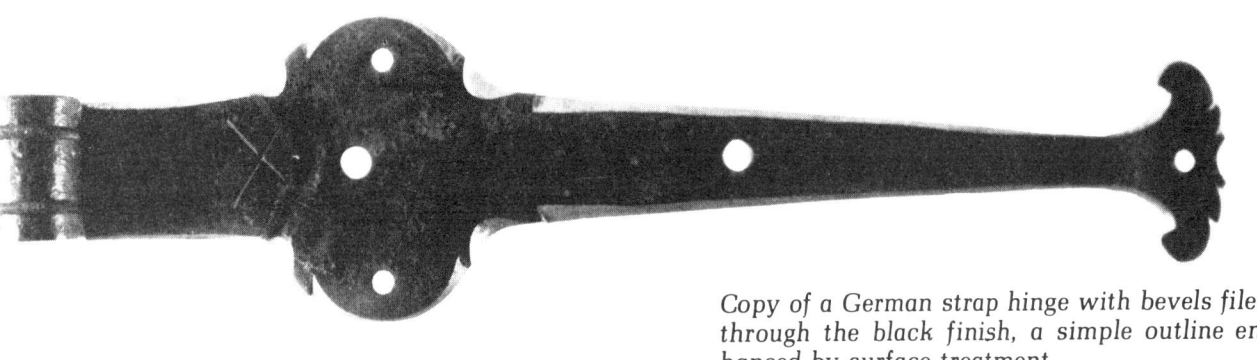

Copy of a German strap hinge with bevels filed through the black finish, a simple outline enhanced by surface treatment.

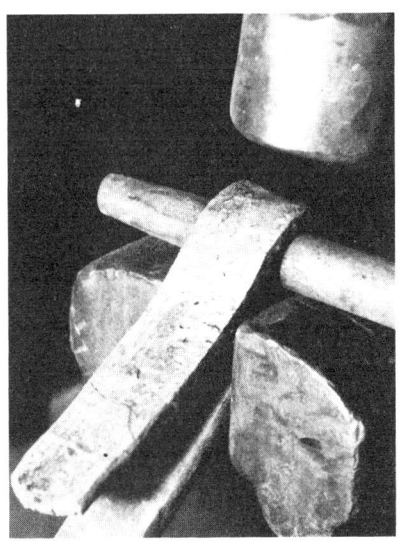

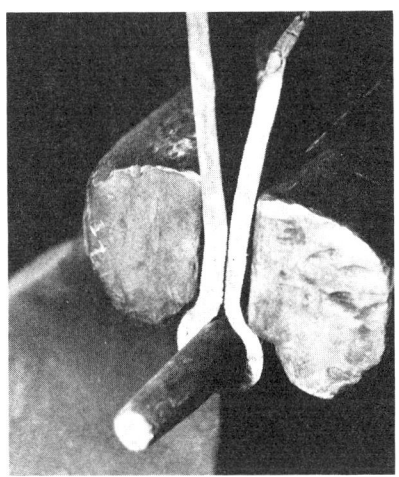

Top, wrapping a pintle collar in the vise; bottom, snugging the iron up to the pin.

The completed hinge leaf described in the preceding section is only half a hinge. It must swing on a hook, a pintle, or some kind of pivot. The pintle is the traditional hook for all but surface hinges such as HL and butterfly. Some pintles are simple bent angles forged in one piece, with one end sharpened to a point and driven into the door frame. Others are forged from two pieces, with a collar welded to a round pin and drawn to a point, sometimes with a round rat-tail brace for decoration and added strength. The one-piece type is strong enough for light hinges such as those for casements, but the two-piece type is better if much weight is to be carried.

To make the two-piece welded pintle, choose material for the spike collar of sufficient weight and size for the eye. The material is to be wrapped hot around a round pin slightly smaller than the finish pin; the pin in these photos is seven-sixteenths inch for a final pin of one-half inch. This can be started over the anvil edge. Since, as we have seen, hot iron curls outward when it is bent, it must be wrapped tightly and snugged up to the pin in order to make a tight weld. One way to do this is to open the vise jaws just wide enough to allow the collar material to swing flatwise, with

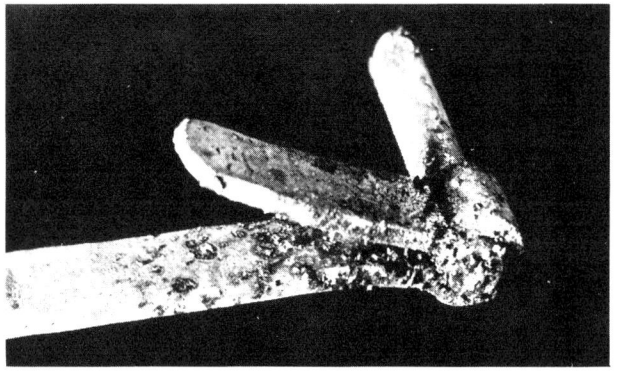

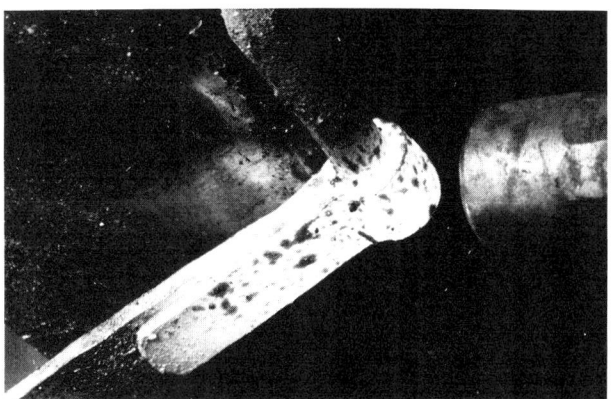

Top, pin in place for welding; bottom, welding the pin.

Top, seating the bearing surface; bottom, the shank drawn.

Barbing the shank.

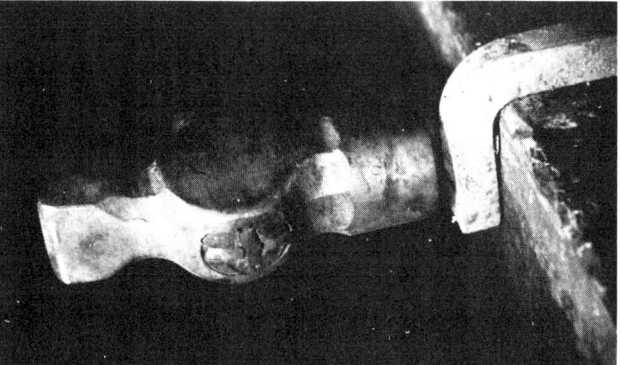

Top, starting one-piece pintle; bottom, upsetting.

the pin thrust through the loop, across the top of the vise. At a good high heat, rotate the iron as the collar is hammered flat against the pin, removing the curl and making a flat ribbon. Do not strike hard enough to reduce the wall thickness.

Make certain the work is hot, then drop it, with pin in place, down between the vise jaws and squeeze the iron up against the pin. A high heat is necessary in order to move the material quickly. Remove the pin by opening the space between the bar and end of the collar. The collar now will tightly hold the finish pin.

Preheat both pieces, add flux to both, and drive the pin into its collar, allowing about one-eighth inch to protrude for welding. Close the joint enough to keep out dirt in the fire and heat for welding. When welding heat is reached, bring the work to the far edge of the anvil, with the shoulder of the collar lying against it, and lightly hammer the collar to weld it to the pin. It is a mistake to think that welding is best done with hard blows. It is not force that unites the two pieces. Heat and clean surfaces do. All the hammer should do at this point is drive out the flux so the union can take place. Forging can be done after the weld is made.

The projecting end of the pin must also be welded, at this heat if possible, but if not, at another. This can be done in any block of steel with the right-size holes, but the bickern made for this purpose is used here. The weld is completed and a bearing seat is forged on the collar at the same time.

To hold the work while drawing the point, after cutting from the bar, fit a pair of tongs for this operation. A ring or link clamped over the ends of the reins will keep the grip tight.

Left, drawing out the corner; right, convenience bend.

Top, rounding the pin; bottom, finished pintle.

Sometimes it is advisable to barb the spikes so they will be less apt to pull out of the wood, particularly when doors or gates may get caught in the wind, or when pintles are to be driven into soft wood. This can be done very quickly when the iron is red by using a sharp hot chisel on the corners with hatchetlike blows. There are times when pintles must be driven through door frames and clinched, the most secure fastening. In such cases the post thickness must be known so that shafts can be forged thin enough to bend at the right places.

The one-piece pintle is much easier to forge. It is forged from square iron, not, as one might assume, from round iron bent at 90°. At the first forging heat make a right-angle bend at the end of the bar for the pin. At a second high heat quench all except the corner and upset into a fairly sharp outside corner. To further strengthen the corner and to assure ample driving surface, forge down the corner in a slope. Bend the bar behind the corner, to provide a working handle in line with the pin end, and forge it to round section. Then straighten the bar, cut off the work, and draw the point.

Starting a strap hinge eye in the bender.

Hinge-Eye Bender

The smith who makes many strap hinges can lighten the work of forming eyes by making benders of such sizes as he needs. They are easily welded together of steel bar stock. A flat bar, a little wider than the width of material for the hinge, one-half inch thick, is the bed, with a flange welded to its base to be held in the vise. A cage holds a movable jaw of tool steel, which can be adjusted with a set bolt, and the assembly welded to a handle.

A removable steel pin slides through holes in ears welded to the base and cage. In use, the hot, or, if thin stock, cold steel flat is fed through the space under the pin and the jaw is tightened against its end. The handle is then pulled up and the steel band is drawn around the pin over a roller set in the base, forming a round eye with flat walls.

The bender can also be used to bend eyes prior to welding, if that is the eye form required for strength. When working hot, the pin is pulled out before hot steel can shrink to it. A bender should be at hand for each size pin, but each can handle material up to its width.

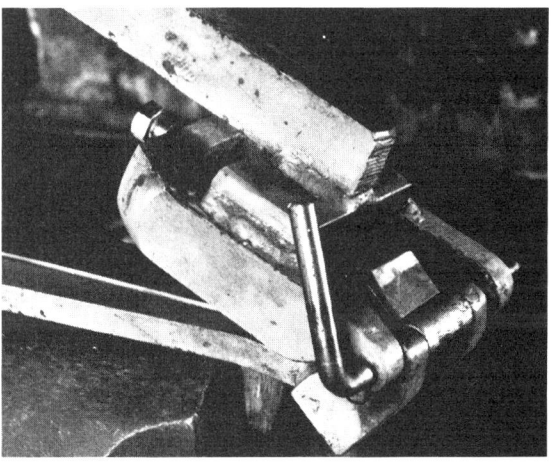

Closing the eye.

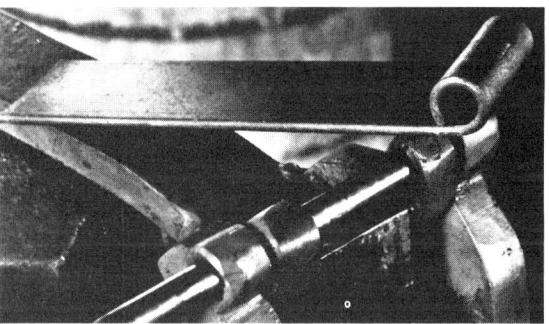

Cold-formed hinge eye.

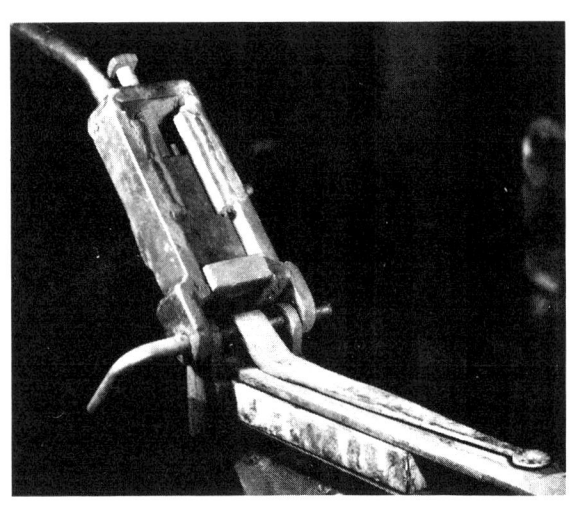
Strap hinge offset bender.

Strap Hinge Offset Bender

In places where doors or shutters have to swing past moldings or brick reveals, hinges must be cranked, or offset, to place the pivot point a little more than half the distance to be cleared.

The offset bender is made on the same principle and in much the same way as the eye bender, by welding steel plates together. The difference is that in this case the bed is set two inches below the eye pin, to give room for blocking up with steel bars to any desired offset. The steel jaw in the cage is now a forming nose, held in any position by a setscrew and adjustment bolt, so that any horizontal distance between eye and bend can be maintained.

In use, a hinge, after being forged flat, is laid in the fire. The eye is brought to a red heat, then chilled to prevent distortion from the pull of the binding. Next, the eye is placed in the bender. The removable pin is inserted, and the handle is pulled down so the nose forms the bend on the steel-plate base. If any hump arises during the bend, it can be hammered flat before the pin is removed. In this way any number of hinges can be offset to the same angle in a very short time. Alternate noses are made for very sharp bends.

Die for rolled hinge joint.

Die for Rolled Hinge Eyes

Some small sheet-iron hinges do not require welded eyes, yet cannot be handled readily in benders. The traditional way to form these cold is to form a die in which to press them. A block of tool steel is drilled and milled to the proper size for the die. The end of the blank is started in the right curve and inserted in the die. In the arbor press, the blank is forced down into the die and rolled around a pin.

If a small, thin hinge is of the strap type, its eye can be cold-rolled in a similar die, modified to suit the hinge. Since the length and thickness of the strap would cause it to bend if not supported, a track is welded to the die face and slotted to allow movement downward but not sideways. The ram is split also, to straddle the track. As the ram moves down, the metal, which is prevented from moving otherwise, is forced into the die to form the eye.

Die and track for small strap hinge eye rolling.

Hinge-Butt Centering Jig

When many hinge-butt eyes must be centered for jamb mounting, they can be done in a jig in the arbor press. The butt, with eye rolled in the eye bender, is set in the jig with a removable pin through the jig and eye. The butt leaf rests on another round pin, which acts as a roller and spacer. The press ram, fitted with a round-nosed punch, neatly forms the bend as the ram descends.

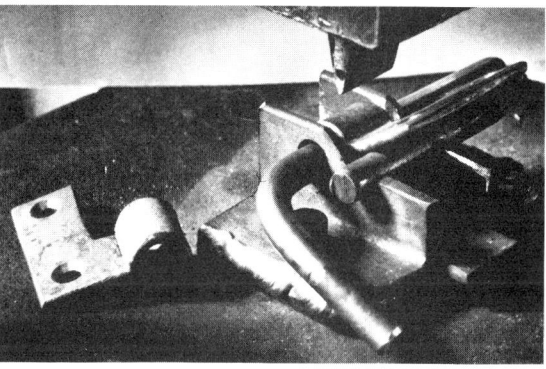

Hinge butt offset bending jig.

WELDED HASP

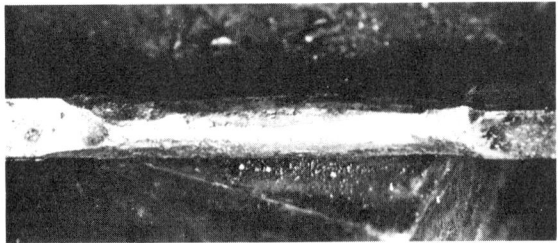

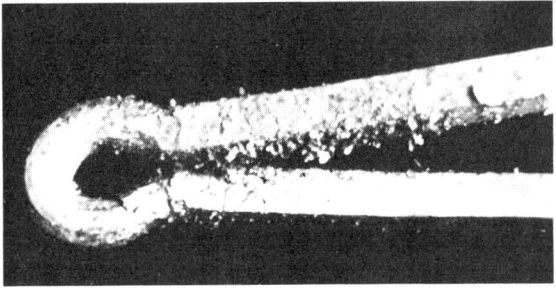

Top, round section for eye; bottom, ready to weld.

To forge this eighteenth-century form of hasp, which requires no hole punching or slotting, use a bar of square stock. To make a hasp eight inches long, forge a round section two inches long, seven and one-half inches from the end.

Bend the round part to form an eye. Behind the eye, weld together the two square bars for a distance of two inches. Then drive a round punch through the eye to round it. Use a yellow heat so the round will follow the punch easily. This also will test your weld. Cut off both pieces at seven and three-quarters inches overall, which will allow enough material to forge the other end.

With the work now held in tongs fitted to hold the eye, bend the ends apart for clearance, and, with the work at the far edge of the anvil, scarf each end to a thin edge on opposite sides. Heat and flux the ends and lap them over each other so that they extend a little past the edges, in case they should slip a little during the weld. Make the weld, and draw the end to a flat taper for a flat scroll.

To form the oval eye, make a special tool called a drift. This need not be made of tool steel, since no cutting or punching will be done. Taper it in width and thickness to the size of your desired eye, with knife edges with which to enter the crack between both welds. File it smooth and symmetrical.

With the work at a good high heat, across the jaws of the vise, drive the tool through and form the eye.

Left, eye rounded; right, blank trimmed to length.

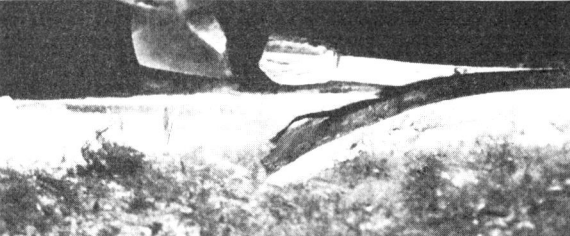

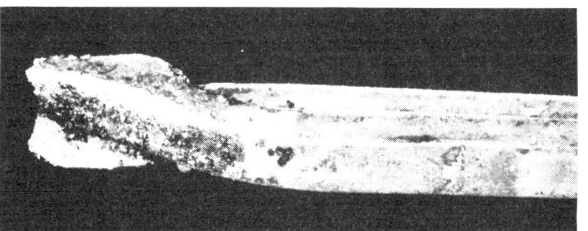

Left, ends scarfed; right, lapped for welding.

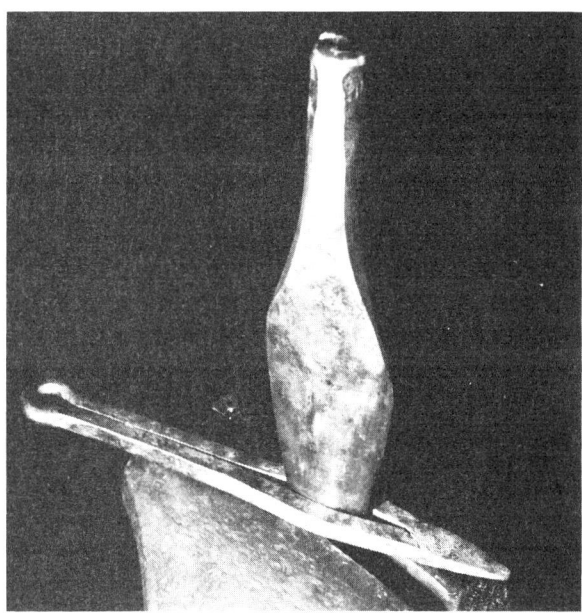

Drift opening the staple eye.   *The staple eye drift.*

Flatten the curved part to increase its width, retaining full thickness at the round eye end, and blend in all transitions. Roll up the tip into a scroll to form a finger grip away from the wood when in use. Make two staples, according to the thickness of the wood where the hasp will be used.

SLOTTED HASP

Drift for slotted-hasp eye.   *Drift cutting the slot.*

When forging hasps with slots for staples, the work of cutting the slots can be facilitated by making a drift to do the work quickly and exactly. To make such a drift, use tool steel of a size equal to the size of the slot—here three-eighths inch by one and one-half inches. Forge the end into a driving handle about seven inches long, for ease of handling. Cut the working end at an angle sharp enough to shear, about 30° from horizontal, leaving a half-inch nub on the long end for a pilot. Grind this to half-round section. Harden and temper to a deep blue.

Lay out the slot on the hasp, and drill three-eighth-inch holes at each end. With the work hot, hold it over the vise jaws, which are opened just enough to clear the tool, and drive the tool through the work from each end. The blade, having been ground to sharp edges, will shear out the slug cleanly. This drift will cut holes or slots up to three inches long. The drift can be made in the time it would take to cut one slot otherwise.

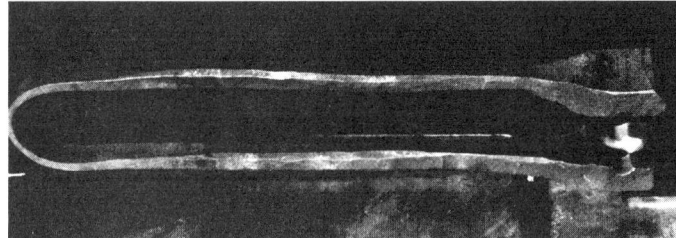

Spring die for small French knob.

Forging in Spring Dies

A smith often is called upon to make work requiring many forged knobs or finials, or ornamental collars welded to round shafts. The best and most economical way to do this is also the most traditional, by the use of spring dies and a power hammer. The spring die is really nothing more than a pair of top and bottom swages joined together with a handle and spring. It has the advantage of always remaining lined up. It is held in one hand by the smith, whose other hand rotates the work in the die while the hammer, or the helper with a sledge, does the striking.

For the relatively small quantities usually required, dies need not be made of tool steel. Since they will form only very hot iron, mild steel will suffice, and it can be worked more easily and cheaply. The one shown above forms a tapered round knob and shaft of eighteenth-century French form. It was used to make bolts for the restoration of the Cabildo in New Orleans.

To make the die, forge a bar of hot-rolled steel, two inches by three-quarters inch, into a blank, with a thin center section to form a spring. Bend the bar to the form shown, so that the heavy die ends meet and line up with each other. Then open it enough for the knob template to enter it, and allow to cool.

Forge the pattern for the knob at the end of a bar long enough to hold without tongs. True it on the

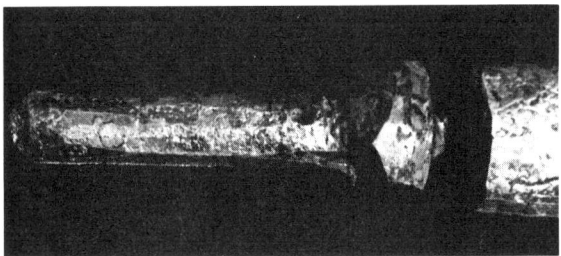

Forged blank for knob.

Knob in die under power hammer.

Finished die forging.

lathe. Heat red hot, and chill. This is done to harden it as much as possible, although being mild steel, it cannot get brittle.

Both pieces are ready to form the die. Place the die blank in the fire and slowly bring up to a high yellow heat, with frequent turning of the work so that both die ends heat equally. When both ends are at the same high heat, take it from the fire and hold in one hand while the other hand positions the pattern between the die faces. Take the work directly to the power hammer, with flat dies in place, and hold as steady as possible. Use the hammer to drive the hot steel down around the pattern. Keep this position until both die faces meet, and the die is made—half impression in each die.

After cooling, some filing will be needed to remove sharp edges that might cut into material being forged. File a groove in each face past the top of the knob cavity to allow room for excess metal squeezed out as the die is used.

To use the die, forge a knob blank at the end of a bar and cut off. Experience will show the proper size of forging that will work best in the die, to fill it with the least waste.

Hold the blank forging in tongs and bring to a yellow heat. Dip the die in water and set the blank in its jaws. Rotate the blank a bit to locate the

Steps in forging a large French knob.

knob in the socket and to remove scale from the work, which in the die would produce a rough surface.

Feed the work into the hammer with round dies in place. Rotate the work in the dies while the hammer drops and forms the knob. The hammer should strike in the center of the dies, to avoid shock to hands from off-center blows. The round faces make this easier than do the flat ones. When the die faces almost meet, remove the work and check it. If it is out of round, reposition it and correct by dropping the hammer a few times.

When knobs of relatively large size with small necks are required, it is easier to make them by welding rather than forging the whole from one piece of large stock. To make the French knob shown, which is one and one-half inches in diameter, with a slim neck, a blank was forged from one-inch round iron to make the neck and a core for the wider part. Then a ribbon of half-round section was forged in a swage and wrapped around the core. Both then were welded together in a spring die and finished in the lathe to match the eighteenth-century original. This sort of lathe turning can be done freehand, as with wood turning, with cutting tools ground from old square files. Patterns, as well as finished work, can be produced this way.

Freehand turning a small knob in the lathe.

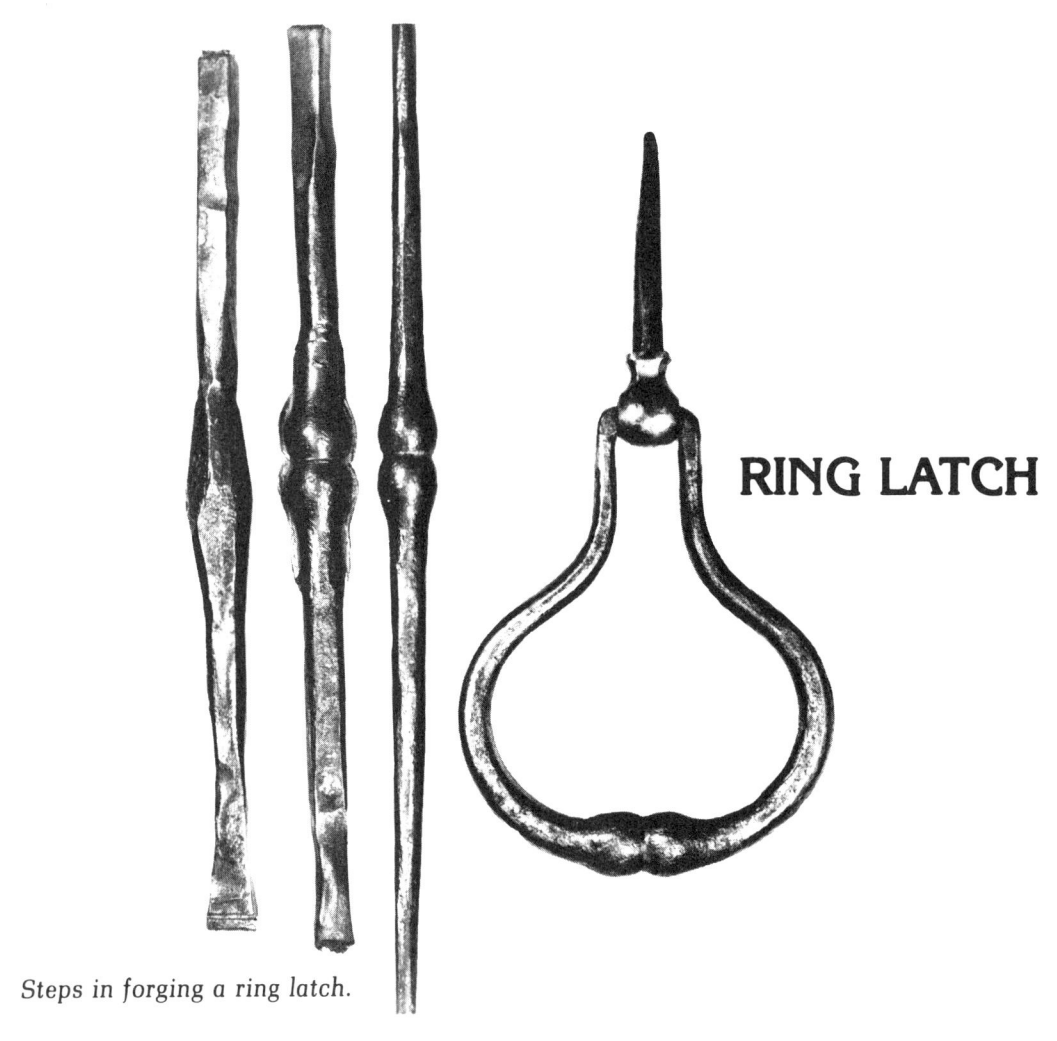

Steps in forging a ring latch.

RING LATCH

To forge this ancient form of ring latch, use five-eighth-inch round stock and roughly forge a blank whose center will fill the spring die made for it, with ends to forge out round. In the spring die, form the center, filing off any flash before finishing in the die. Draw the ends to equal lengths and sections, tapering in diameter to the ends, which would be about one-quarter inch round.

Bend each end at right angles, scarf and weld them, and file the section round. After welding, finish shaping the ring, which is impossible to do without the weld. The door shaft is wrapped, not welded, in order to allow split ends for clinching through a latch bar. See the shop drawings for a latch of similar form.

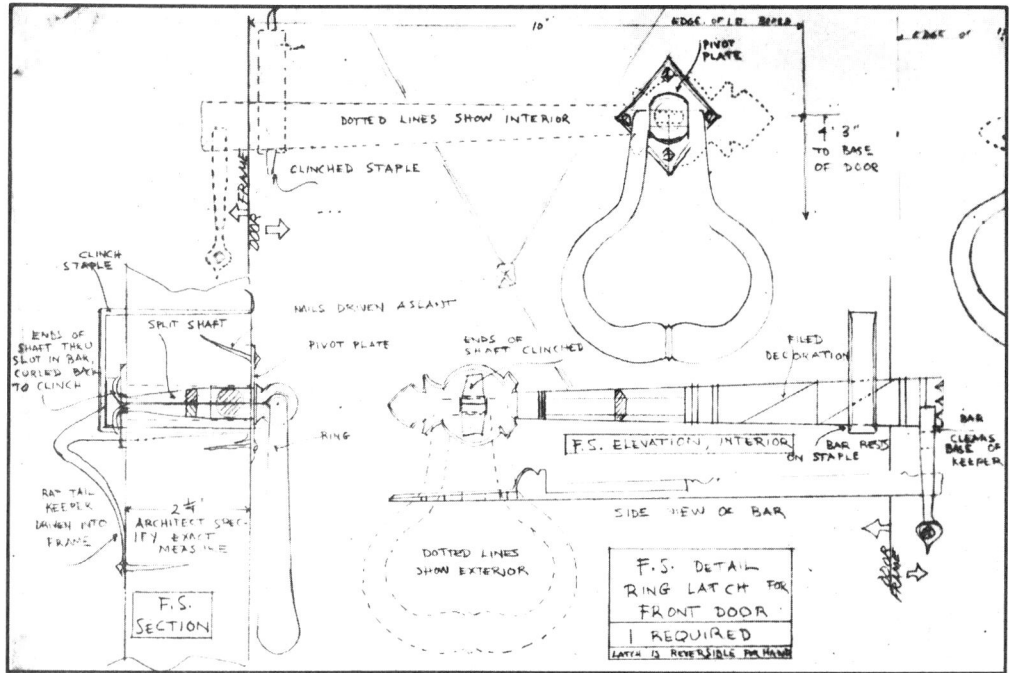

Shop drawing for a ring latch, seventeenth-century English form.

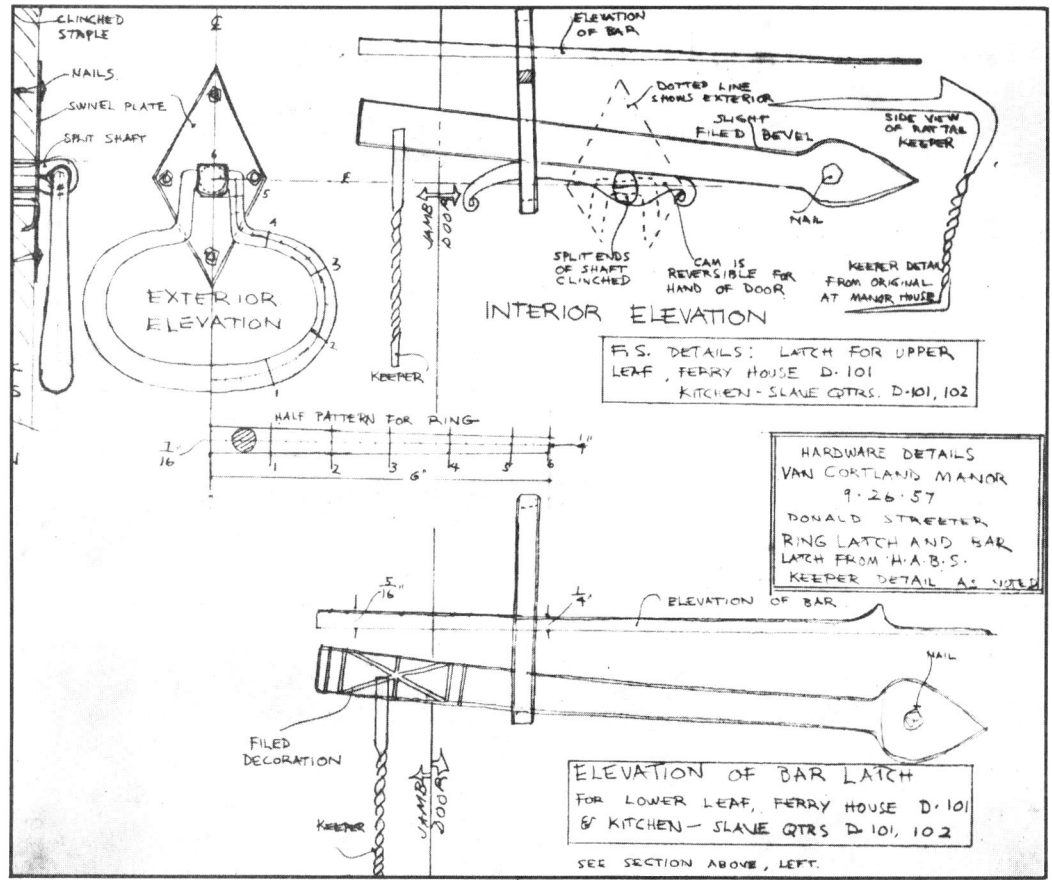

Shop drawing for a ring latch, eighteenth-century Dutch form.

Forged spring end of iron bolt.

Spring end bent for welding.

Forging the grasp.

Bending the grasp.

Spring Bolts

These usually are of two kinds: those with integrally forged iron springs, and those with welded steel ones. They have the advantage over plain slide bolts in that they will stay in either locked or unlocked position when used vertically or horizontally, because of the spring. The iron-spring type is older, made before rolling mills produced square bar iron, and was forged from hammered rectangular bars. Both kinds were mounted on plates. They moved between staples, with locking notches to engage one staple and prevent unlocking except from the bolt side of the door.

To make the iron spring bolt, choose a flat bar of suitable size. At the end of the bar, draw out a thin taper, the length of the bolt shaft. Make it very thin at its end and somewhat wider in its center, to form the dog-ear stops, which will prevent the bolt from escaping its staples. Leave a sharp corner at the bar end of the taper—here reduced to half the bar thickness—and at that point cut it nearly through. Bend it back against the bar and weld both together back for about one inch. This completes the spring.

Allowing enough material for forging a bend and scroll, cut from the bar. Depending upon bolt size, three-eighths inch will be enough for the bend, and one inch for the scroll. With the work in tongs, forge a neck past the bend point, and form a wedge-shaped end with rounded corners. Spread this out crosswise with the cross-peen, then finish

Starting the scroll.

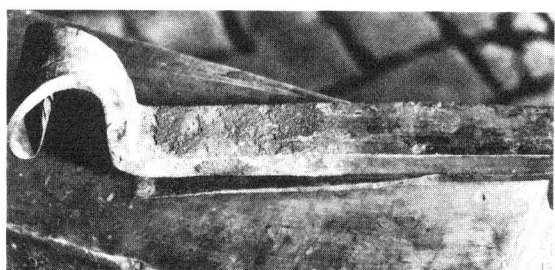
The forged bolt.

Trimming the spring for dog-ear stops.

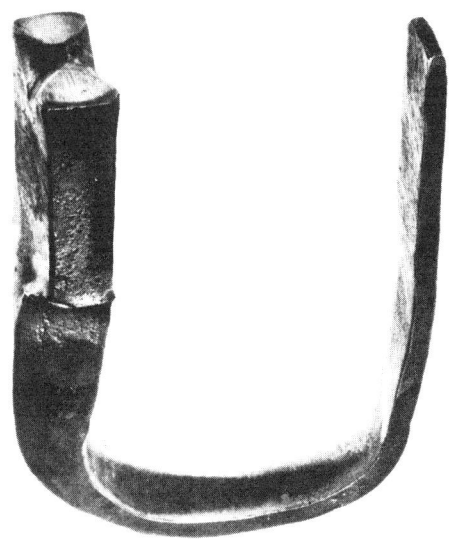
Vise anvil and gauge for forging steel spring ears.

the form on the horn and anvil, smoothing and refining the curves, and file to finish form.

At a good high heat, lock the bolt in the vise and make the bend, away from the spring, seeing that the bend is at right angles to the bolt, so the scroll end will stand upright. True any distortion while hot.

Turn the bolt bottom side up on the anvil. With an edge of the hammer face, strike a series of blows crosswise, starting at the thin edge of the spring and progressing back to the weld. The spring will rise up in a curve away from the shaft. Because of its taper, the spring will maintain tension no matter what position it takes within its staples.

To make the dog-ear stops, lock the bolt in the bench vise, and using one jaw-top edge as a shear, saw slots at the sides of the ears. Use a sharp cold chisel to cut away the excess metal. File all rough edges of the spring, which might affect its smooth action, and finish file the shaft and locking notch.

Forging spring ears in the vise.

Spring and bolt ready for welding.

Curving the spring for tension.

The forging technique for the steel spring bolt is similar, except for a change in scroll design and the use of square iron. If a number of springs are to be made, make a tool-steel jig to forge all the dog-ears instead of having to forge each one over a corner of the anvil. Using one-half-inch by one-inch tool steel, forge a long leg and bend it into a U shape. It should fit in the vise with its end standing higher than the flat anvil part, to form a gauge for length and to position each spring blank for forging the ears. File the top of the anvil surface so as to leave the spring at full thickness at its center while the hammer draws out the two ears at once.

Preheat the heavier bolt shank to orange, and the spring to red, and flux both. With the work positioned in side-gripping tongs and the spring on top, take a welding heat. Take it from the fire and quickly draw the underside, which will be the bolt face, across a wire brush to remove the scale. Make the weld.

Curl the spring and file to shape. No tempering will be necessary, since high-carbon steel will have enough tension without it, and very little movement is involved.

Rat-Tail Keeper for Latch Bar
At the end of a bar of one-quarter-inch by three-quarter-inch iron, over the edge of a straight-sided fuller, forge a notch about three-eighths inch deep. Draw the notched end out into a square-pointed spike. Over a fuller of rather broad radius, thin the iron behind the remaining edge of the notch into a flat ribbon. Cut the piece from the bar at an angle along the curve. Forge the ribbon flat and true, leaving a heavier, pointed end.

On the anvil, with the cross-peen, spread out the end of the ribbon to form a spear finial, thinning the edges, but holding strength at the center.

If many of these keepers are to be made, alter a pair of heavy, flat-lip tongs by cutting off one lip five-eighths inch from its end and squaring it. Grind the end of the other lip to a curve that falls away from the top edge.

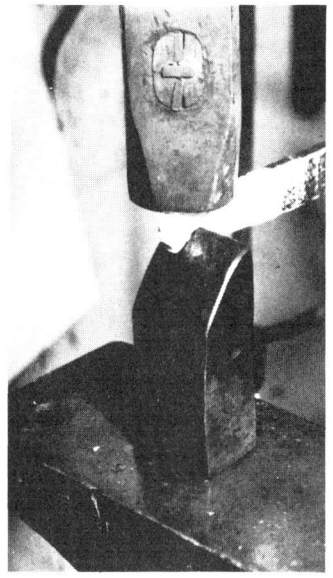

Left, fullering for shaft; right, fullering for neck.

Cutting the blank from the bar.

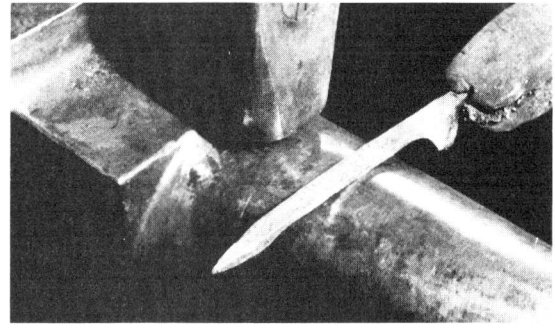

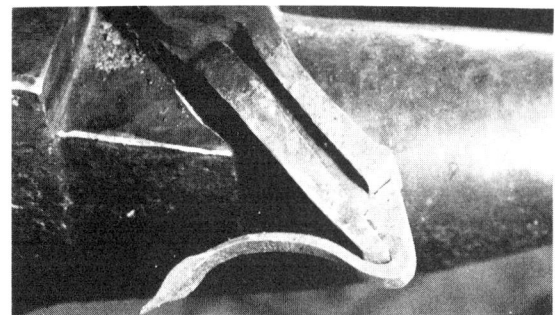

Top, thinning the neck; bottom, forging the finial.

Top, sharpening the inside angle and dressing the slope; bottom, bending the rat-tail in the tongs.

Grasp the piece by the spike and bring to a yellow heat. Hold it firmly in these special tongs and upset the slope against the end of the top lip to form a plane slope and sharp inside corner. Bend the rat-tail down against the bottom lip and form its curve. Very little filing will finish the part.

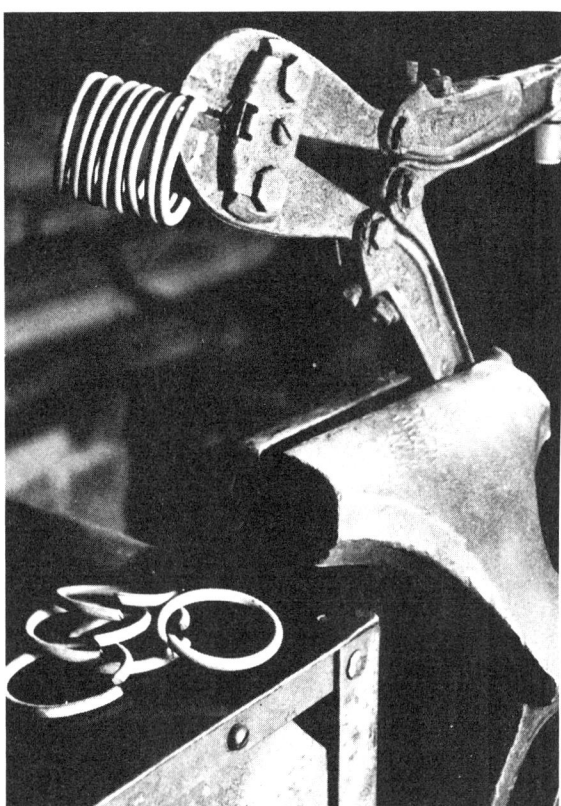

Cutting wire rings from a coil.

Rounding the ring with a mandrel.

Forming Welded Wire Rings

To form quantities of identical wire rings, wrap the wire around a suitable mandrel in a spring-like spiral, and cut them apart with bolt clippers. Make the cuts at an angle, which will provide enough scarfing to make the welds without pre-forging. All that is needed is to lap the joints.

As with most rings of this sort, the weld is made flatwise, not over the horn, to avoid stretching. The sides of the weld, however, are dressed there. It is impractical to try to round welded wire rings from the outside. It is better to use a tapered mandrel and a bolster, and round them hot from the inside. A mark or ledge on the mandrel will help to size them alike.

Forming Split Eyes

When a great many identical eyes must be made, of the type not welded, but tapered for clinching through wood, it will pay to make a simple bending fork for that job. Using round steel of the size needed for the eye, bend it into U form and lock it in the vise. Forge the work to a determined length. Hold it in the tongs and bend around one pin, while the other pin holds it in place. Center the eye and equalize the legs by blows of the cross-peen, first on one side and then the other, turning the eye on the pin for proper bearing.

Forming split eyes on a vise-held U fork.

The hook jig.

Bending Jig for Hooks

When many hooks must be made alike, as for shutters for a large building, make a bending jig rather than bending them over the anvil horn, which is not the best place for such bends. On the anvil the bend is made downward, so the curve you make is out of view, and control is lost. It is better to make such bends horizontally, where you can see them form and maintain control.

The bending jig can be made simply of flat stock. Faggot-weld a tail into a shaft for the hardy hole. Fit the flat top of the jig with two riveted studs to control the bend. Make the right-angle bend at the anvil. Heat the work to a yellow, drop it in place, and form the bend rapidly.

Bending hooks in an anvil jig.

Jig for Bending Offsets in Flat Stock

Neck bolts must be made with offsets in the shaft, to fit in mortises away from doorstop edges. To make such bends all alike in any quantity, make a jig to hold the work in the vise. Weld a piece of flat steel the thickness of the offset to one end of another bar, and braze or weld straps to it to bend around the vise jaws to keep it in place. In use, the bolt shaft is heated and locked in place with a first bend against the spacer and the end of the vise. Pry the end away from the jaw with a hot cutter and then hammer it against the spacing block. Finish by upsetting the corner on the anvil.

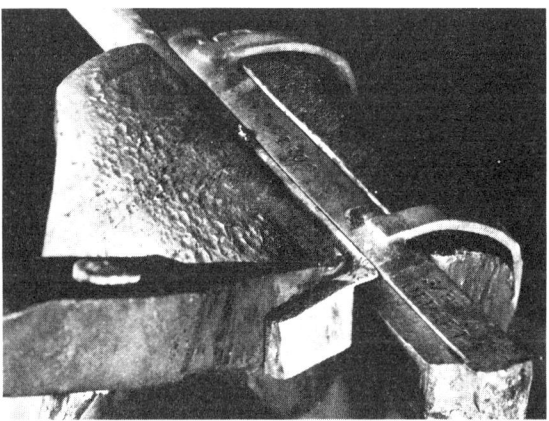

Jig for bending offset bolt shafts.

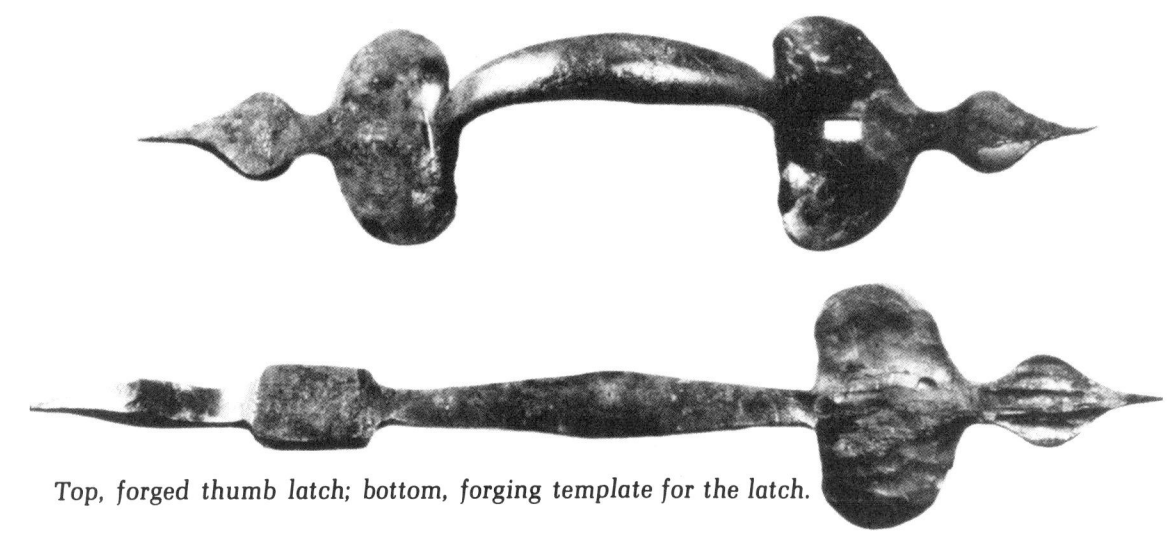

Top, forged thumb latch; bottom, forging template for the latch.

Forging templates for a shutter dog.

Forging Templates

If you plan to forge work such as hardware or domestic decorative pieces in quantities, or expect repeat orders of the same items, you should assure yourself of some means to duplicate later what you make today. Card files and shop photographs help to maintain this kind of quality control, but one of the best ways to refresh the memory is to make and keep forging templates of all such items.

Whenever possible, the template should record several bits of information. A thumb-latch template, for instance, should tell you the size of the original stock, the rough forging, and at least some of the finished forms. Measurements not possible to keep in the template can be recorded in the card file.

Customers may reorder, years later, and will expect the new work to match the old. A friend may see an item, and want to order some like it, which is the best sort of advertising you can ever have.

Tinned casement latch, seventeenth-century English form.

Bender for small pulls.

Tinning

Many seventeenth-century small iron pieces were coated with tin as a preservative against rust. These pieces included hardware and nails, which were exposed to dampness.

To tin by hot dipping, first clean the surface of all scale, oil, or grease, and rub it well with Sal Ammoniac for flux. Melt block tin in a vessel on the forge, not hot enough to form a blue oxide on the surface, but just enough to liquefy it. Scrape away any scum from the top, and slip the work quickly into the bath with fine-tipped tongs. Hold it there long enough for it to reach the same heat as the molten tin. Remove it, and quickly tap it to shake off any surplus tin that may form lumps. A bright, attractive finish will remain on the work. Pieces that are made up of more than one unit should be dipped before assembly so they don't become soldered together.

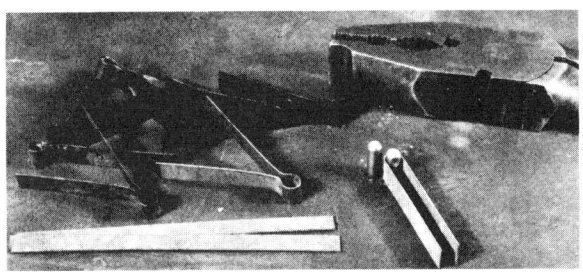
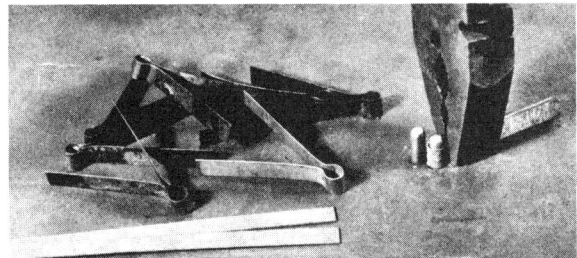
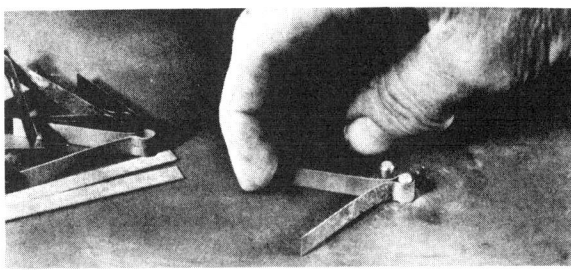

Steps in forming small springs.

Template for trimming, bending, and filing springs for a spring latch.

Forming and Tempering Small Springs

When a quantity of small scissors springs are to be made, form them in a simple jig consisting of two round steel pins of the right diameter set into holes in a steel plate, and spaced so as to allow passage between them of the spring-steel blank. Bend the spring at the center around one pin into a U shape. Use pliers to snug both ends up against the pin. Pivot the spring around one pin and bend each leg to its correct angle. Harden and temper in oil.

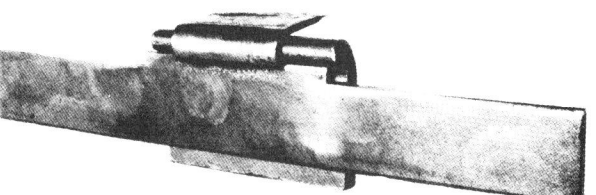

Form for starting H-hinge eye bends.

Template for scribing and trimming H hinges, with a trial pin as reference point.

Jig for clamping door knob parts while silver soldering.

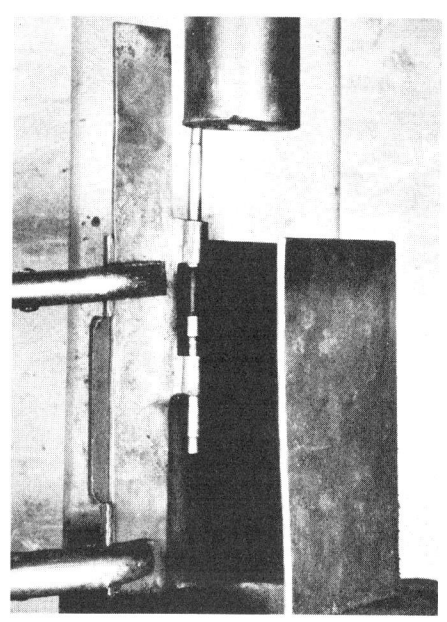

Jig for clearing and rounding H-hinge eyes.

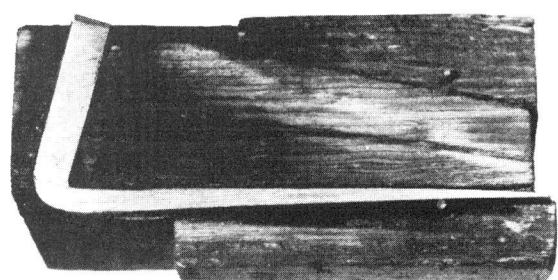

Wooden jig for holding latch springs while finishing on the sanding belt.

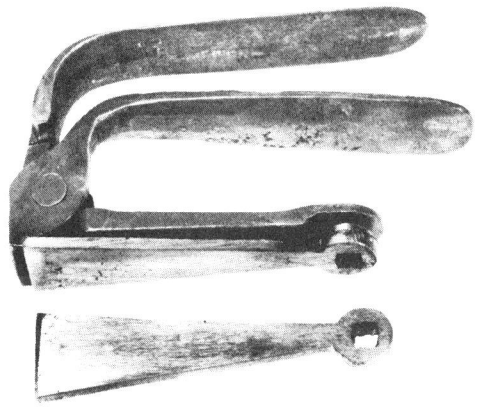

Tool for holding latch bars on the belt sander.

NORFOLK LATCH

A Norfolk latch is one in which the grasp is riveted to a backplate, as opposed to a Suffolk latch, in which grasp and cusps are forged from the same bar. Whereas the Suffolk latch can be almost completed at the anvil with no special tools, the Norfolk is a more sophisticated form, requiring forging dies and punches. It was developed in the early years of the nineteenth century in one of the first efforts at industrialization in the English hardware trade. Smiths hand forged the latch, but they used the then-current technology of the rolling mills, which produced sheet iron that did not need to be hammered out.

The latch shown here is a simple form of the Norfolk type. Characteristic of the style is the round handle with decorative center collar and shoulders to strengthen the joint at grasp and plate. Special tools were made to fabricate all parts. The collar in this one does not completely encircle the handle, and requires two anvil die swages to form it.

The first is a forming die to bend the collar around the round handle stock. Make it from a piece of mild steel, one and one-half inches square, and forge with a shank to fit the hardy hole. Heat it to a high heat, and hammer into it a preforged template the size and form of your collar, producing a mold in the steel block.

To make the blanks for the collars, forge a strip of one-inch by one-quarter-inch stock, beveled on each edge to form a truncated pyramid section about one and three-sixteenths inch wide by one-eighth inch thick at the edges. Shear the strip into pieces one and one-sixteenth inch long.

Heat and wrap the collar blank around a mandrel of five-sixteenths-inch round bar, starting the bend in the corner of the anvil table, and snugging it up in the forming swage. The end of the mandrel is relieved to undersize so the collar can be slipped off after it is formed. Since this type of latch, because of the special set-ups and tools it requires, is seldom made one at a time, several parts of each kind should be made at one session.

Cut five-sixteenths-inch round rods to a length somewhat longer than finish size, to allow trimming to exact length later. A second swage is needed to weld the collar and impress the face of the collar at the same time. Forge a template for the collar and file to finish form. In the same way the first swage was made, forge a second one. With the swage block again at a high heat, drive the template into it, taking great care this time that the template remains always in the same spot, in order to make a clear impression.

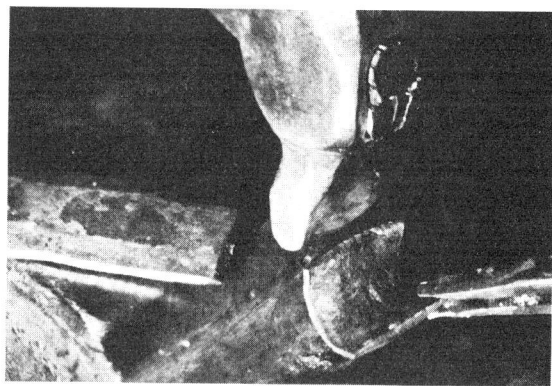

Starting the collar bend.

Forming the collar on a mandrel.

The collar ready for welding.

The anvil die and welded collar.

The blank and the rod must now be assembled, hot and fluxed. Take a welding heat. With the collar pinched to hold it in place, bring it to the die swage, position it in the center, and with a heavy hammer and few blows, keeping the work firmly in position to avoid a double impression, weld all together. The surplus metal will form a flange that can be ground off later. Clean the die of scale after each weld, and cool it after every few welds. With all parts ready to weld, any number can be done in the same way.

Since all grasps should be made to fit identical backplates, and to avoid having to fit them one by one, the rods, with their collars welded, now should be cut to equal lengths. An adjustable rod cutter is used, with the reference point for the gauge being the edges of the welded bands. This will center them in each finished handle.

To forge the shoulders at the ends of the grasps, two special tools are needed: a spring clamp for upsetting, and a spring die for forging. The clamp is made in the same way as spring dies, except that the work is held in the vise instead of under the hammer. The two parts of the die for the clamp are flame cut from mild steel, with ledges left to rest atop the vise jaws, riveted to a strip of spring steel, and bent into position. After fitting to the vise jaws, a hole, slightly under five-sixteenths-inch diameter, is drilled through their meeting

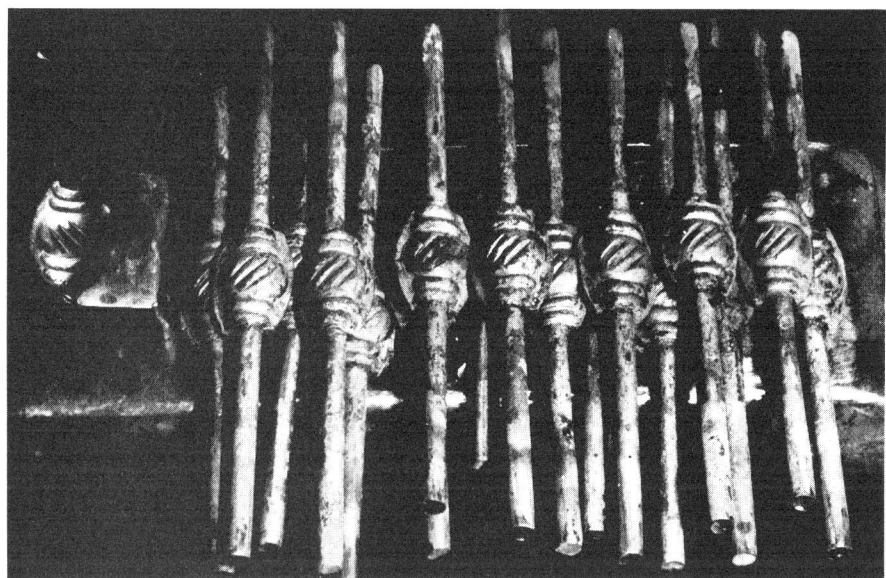

Collars welded.

Trimming the ends.

Spring clamp for upsetting ends.

Upsetting ends in the vise.

joint. In use, the work is brought to high heat, inserted in the clamp with three-quarter inch protruding, locked tightly in place, and the end upset. Some experimenting will determine the amount of upsetting needed. The spring allows quick release of the work. Each end is upset in the same way. As with all such upsetting tools, the top is ground on a slope away from the hole, to provide hammer clearance.

A spring die then is used to forge the upset ends into shoulders. Enough stock is provided in the upsetting to form a stud at the end for riveting to the plate, as the metal is forced out into the chan-

Upset end, with collar and stud formed in spring die.

Attaching the cheeks.

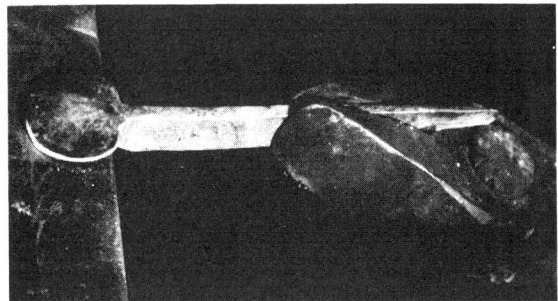

Position of tongs in holding thumb press.

nel made for that purpose. A little filing will fit them to their holes.

After all grasps are forged, bend them to shape over the horn. Grind all flanges to finish form. Use a backplate to fit the studs, and check to see that they seat properly.

To make the plates, several punches with dies are needed. Corner notches and screw holes are punched with stock punches, but a special set must be made to punch the H-shaped slot to receive the cheeks that hold the swivel pin for the thumb press. Make these by filing and riveting or welding together pieces of tool steel, and hardening and tempering them to a mid-blue. Another punch-and-die set is made to make the cheeks, which are blanked from a strip of 14-gauge sheet steel. See illustrations on pages 27 and 28.

To set them in place, one is first placed in the side notch, locked in the vise, and riveted down against the face of the plate. Then, using a spacer of steel the width of the center part of the slot, position the second cheek and lock all together in the vise and rivet down as before.

With both cheeks assembled on the back side of the plate, fit the handle to its stud holes and rivet in place on the face of the backplate.

The thumb press, which moves the latch bar on the opposite side of the door, is made from round stock of suitable size—in this case five-sixteenths inch. Forge a flat section long enough to go through the door and allow lifting, thick enough to pass easily through the cheeks, and thinner at its end. Allowing about one-half inch of round stock, cut from the bar. Upset the end to set the corners and increase size. With tongs grasping the flat part from below to avoid slippage, forge a flat oval for the press. Bend the tip down into a curve, and dish the press on a bottom fuller or other suitable form. File and fit to the latch by drilling a hole through the cheeks and lift to take a small pin. Rivet the pin in place for the swivel.

Many Norfolk latches have collars that entirely surround the handles, and these require some-

Die and forged ribbon for round collar blanks.

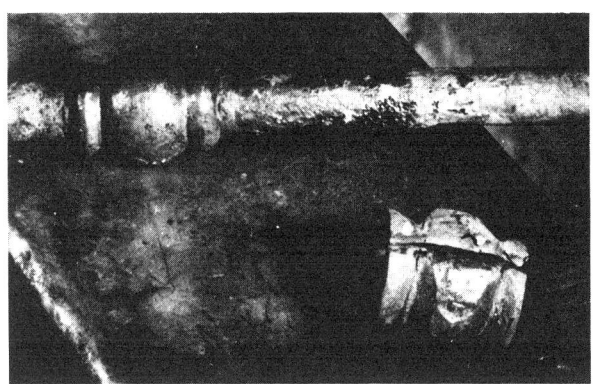

Forged collar and rolled blank.

Curved shear blade and die for fleur-de-lis plate ends.

what different forging than this one. Depending on the size of the round handle and the form of the collar, make an anvil die, or swage, to form a ribbon, whose profile matches that of the intended collar. Make a spring die by forming it on a lathe-turned template, to weld and shape the collar on the handle.

Some experimenting will be necessary in order to arrive at just the right thickness and length for the collar blanks, in order to just fill the die, yet avoid ridges in the curves or creeping of excess metal out along the handle. As with all collar blanks, they should be cut with ends at angles on a radius from the center of the circle.

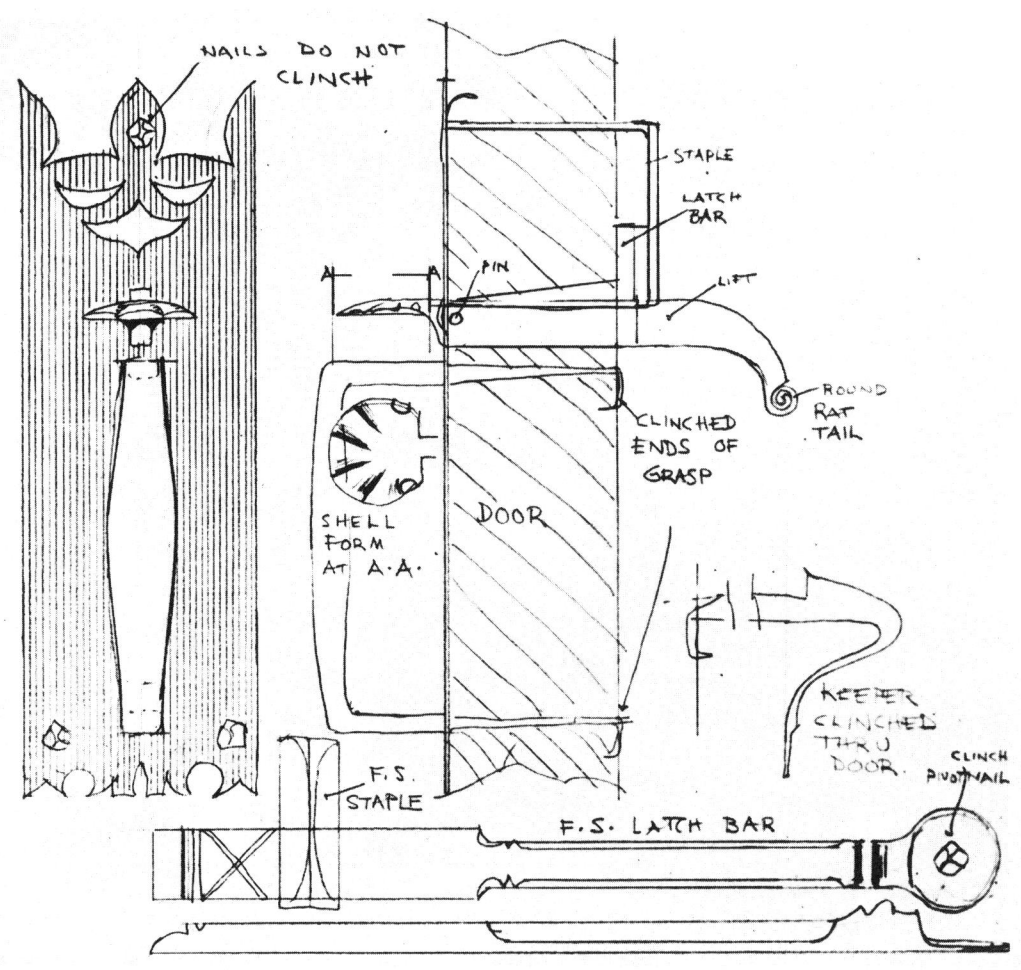

Shop drawing for a Norfolk latch of medieval form.

Some Norfolk latches also have more ornate backplates, requiring more than stock round punches to produce. One design incorporates a fleur-de-lis top, with the same curves repeated at the base. To make these plates, a special shearing blade and die is made, allowing a strip of sheet steel to pass under the blade to a gauge stop. Thus, shearing produces two ends at one stroke. A round punch completes the fleur-de-lis shape.

6 LOCK WORK

Interior of twelve-inch English-type rim lock, backplate removed.

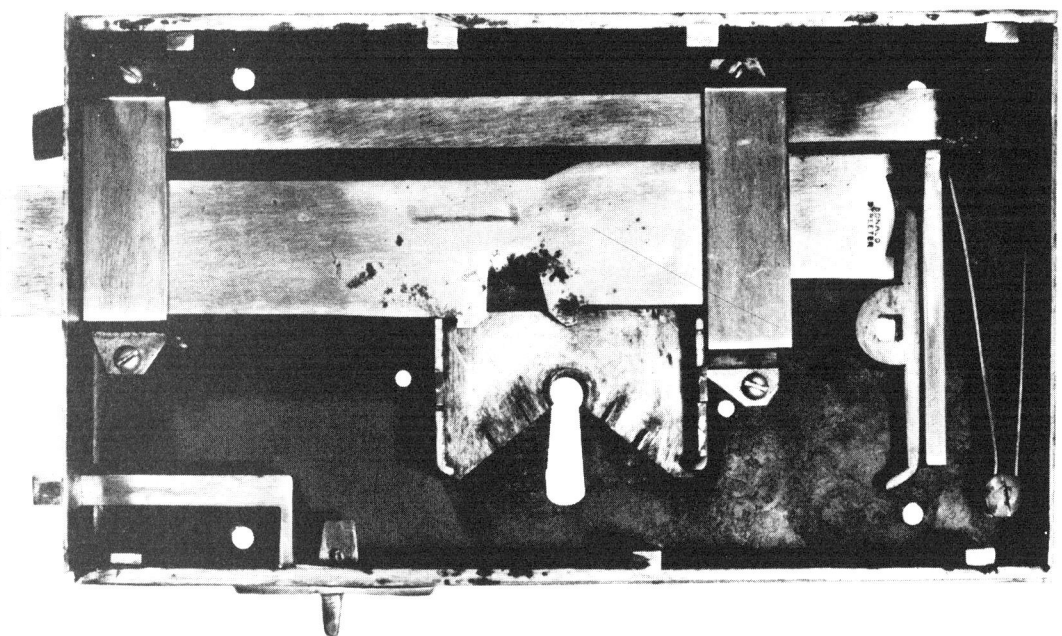

ENGLISH IRON RIM LOCK

A lock, even in basic form, is a minimachine, with accurately fitted parts that move when activated by a key. It must be so constructed that only those elements that are intended to move can do so, thus stabilizing the mechanical movements in their intended paths.

The key is the heart of the lock, and its beginning; from its measurements all other dimensions stem. This may seem strange, but it is logical. By first making the key, the locksmith has a gauge with which to try the movements as he fits the lock together. The security of the lock depends upon the impediments that the wards can put in the way of a false key, but through which the true key can pass. Although no traditional warded

Interior of case, showing stud construction.

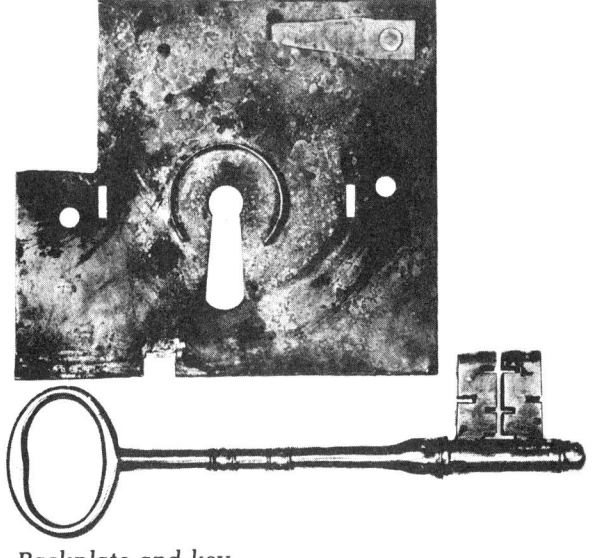

Backplate and key.

locks are pickproof by modern standards, during their time they were the best protection the craft could offer, with endless varieties of shapes, wards, and devices. Some medieval keys and their boxes of wards could be compared to passing one fine-toothed comb through another.

In locks for passage doors, which must be able to be locked from either side, some means must be taken to assure that the key will rest in its proper position each time it is thrust into the lock either way. With keys with bits of symmetrical profile in section, this is done by providing a collar or shoulder behind the bit, which bears against the lock case or backplate, centering the key in its correct place.

To make the key, first forge a blank of proper size, leaving a round section at one end to receive the bit and a flat part at the other for the bow. Split the flat end, bend the parts, and weld into a ring. Bend the rough bow aside and lathe-turn the stem and shaft to proper size. The bit should be made and fitted to the lock before spending time filing the bow, since if the bit fails, all filing time would be wasted.

Because of the shoulder at the base of the stem, it would be difficult to file the sides of the bit after they are fitted, without damaging the collar. So

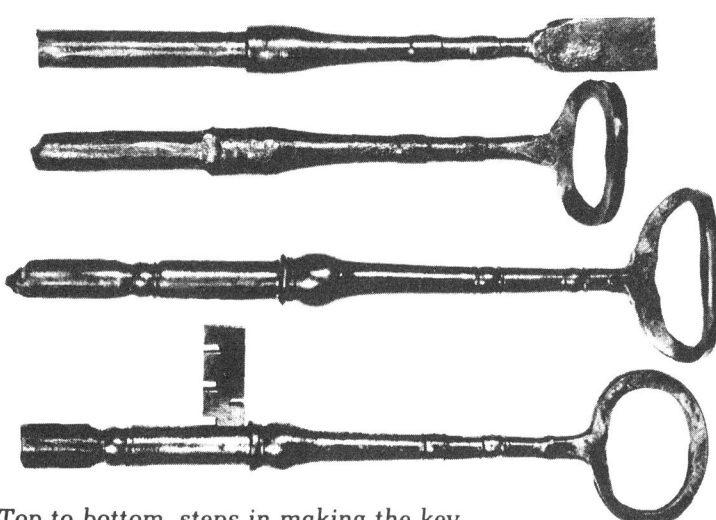

Top to bottom, steps in making the key.

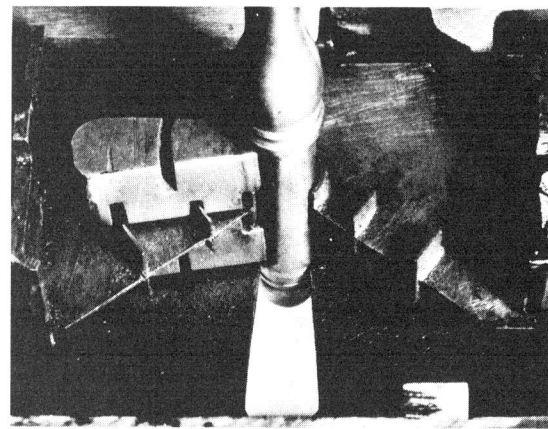

Key moving in the box of wards.

the bit is filed to shape before being attached to the stem. Two identical pieces must be made, with equally spaced clefts to pass the intended wards of the lock. They can take almost any form, provided they do not weaken the bit or allow passage of a bent wire pick strong enough to move the bolt and raise the tumbler.

In this case, the key is cut so as to pass a main center ward and collar, two minor wards, and one continuous ward. Ideally, all clefts should be cut as arcs concentric with the center of the stem, to avoid weakening the bit and to keep the tolerances as close as possible. They can be sawed straight and curved with chisels, or cut in the lathe. In the absence of a lathe, these were done in a jig at the drill press with hole saws of graduated sizes. The two pieces are attached to the stem with tenons, here one-eighth-inch round steel pins, fitted into holes in the stem and bits, and the whole brazed together after clamping, with a spacer sheet between them for the main ward passage. Final finishing was done with thin, sharp cold chisels.

The key made, the lock itself is laid out on a steel sheet that is to be the lock case—here 16-gauge thickness—using prick punch, dividers, and scriber. The box of wards also is laid out in

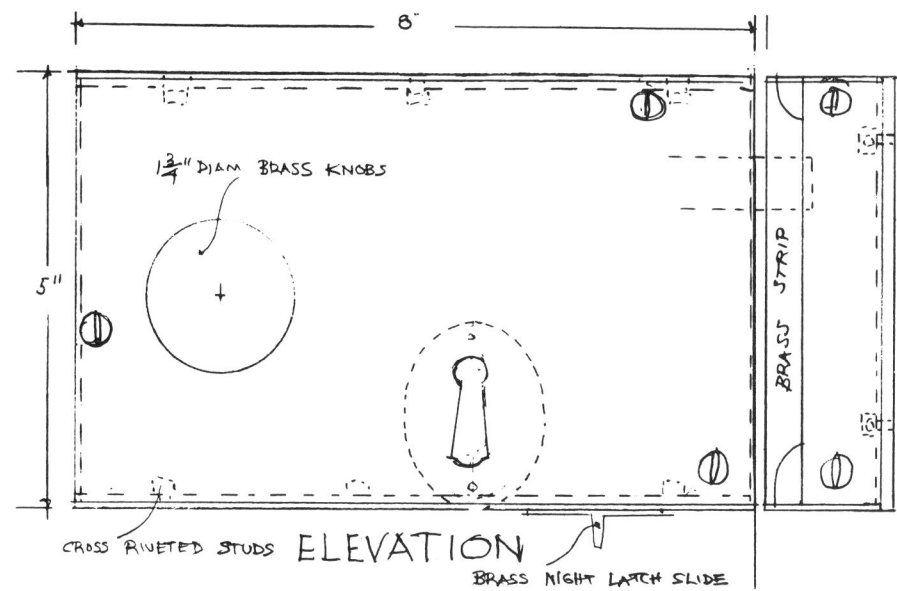

Above, below, opposite: shop drawings for iron rim lock.

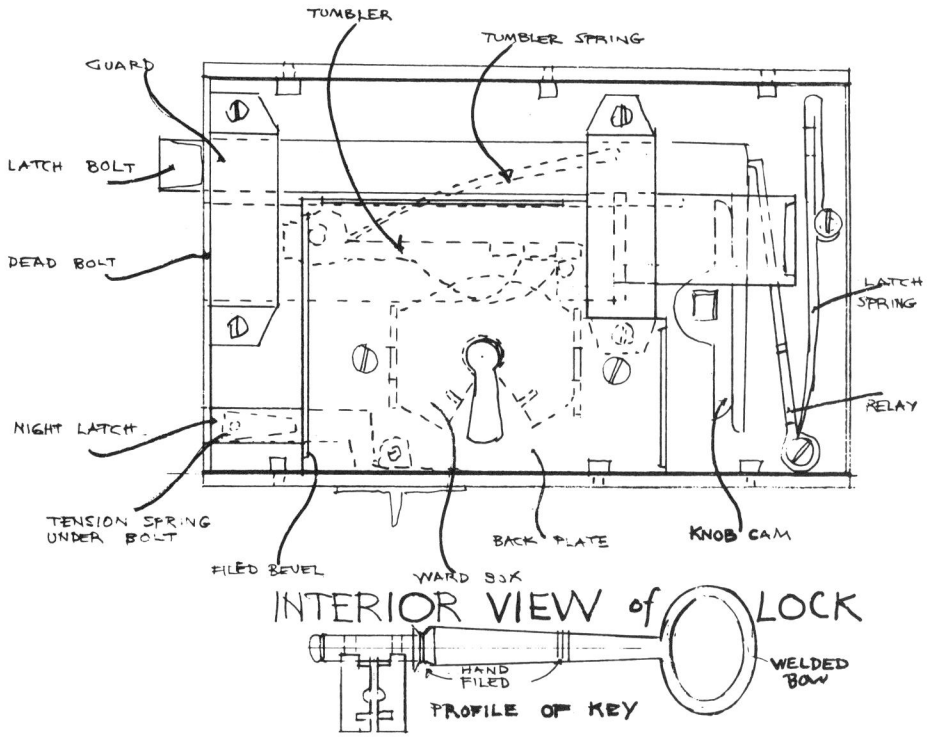

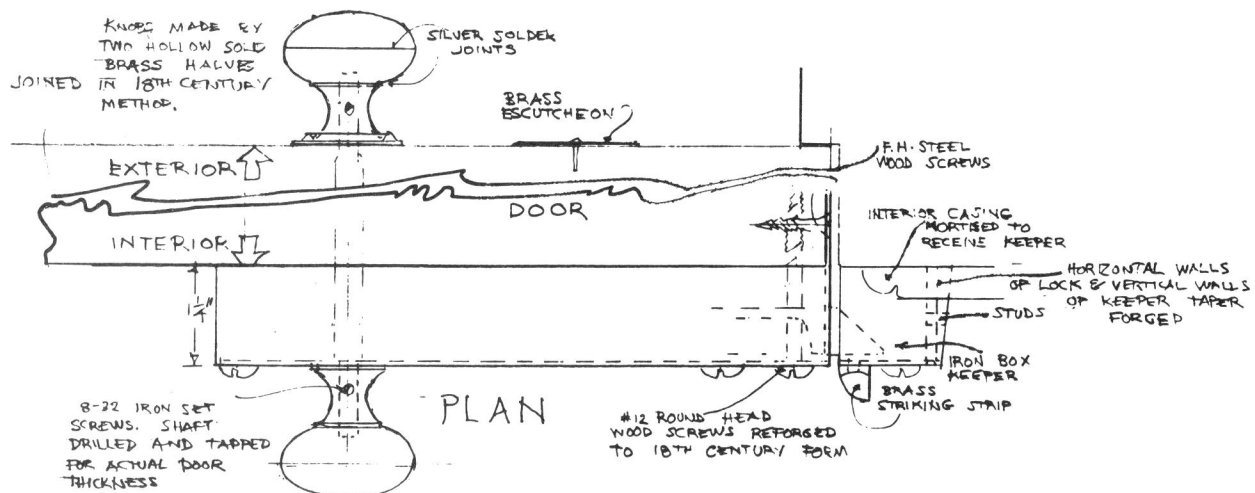

KNOBS MADE BY TWO HOLLOW SOLD BRASS HALVES JOINED IN 18TH CENTURY METHOD.

SILVER SOLDER JOINTS

BRASS ESCUTCHEON

EXTERIOR

INTERIOR

DOOR

PLAN

F.H. STEEL WOOD SCREWS

INTERIOR CASING MORTISED TO RECEIVE KEEPER

HORIZONTAL WALLS OF LOCK & VERTICAL WALLS OF KEEPER TAPER FORGED

STUDS

IRON BOX KEEPER

BRASS STRIKING STRIP

8-22 IRON SET SCREWS. SHAFT DRILLED AND TAPPED FOR ACTUAL DOOR THICKNESS

#12 ROUND HEAD WOOD SCREWS REFORGED TO 18TH CENTURY FORM

identical form, along with the backplate. The main center-ward plate is cut to match them. Tenons are centered at its sides to enter slots cut into the sides of the box, and its center collar and minor wards are silver-soldered in place. Slots are punched in the main and backplates for tenons on the sides of the box, the ward system assembled with trial bolts, and the key filed as need be to make a matching fit while moving easily from either side of the lock. This done, the rest of the parts can be forged and fitted and the lock completed.

The lock illustrated is a three-bolt lock, with latch bolt, dead bolt, and night bolt. It is what is known as a once-dead lock, since one revolution of the key throws the bolt through its entire travel. Some locks were made with two turns of the key required for full bolt movement, enabling the use of smaller keys, easier to carry about, and were called twice-dead locks. The stock lock shown on page 119 is of that type.

In this lock, the dead bolt and latch bolt were faggot-welded of flat stock in the traditional method, to avoid having to forge down heavier stock for the thin sections. Two saw cuts were made in the lower edge of the main bolt, in position for the key to strike, and the center part bent down at a right angle to form a talon. This talon engages behind a similar talon on the tumbler when in unlocked position, and ahead of it when locked. The tumber is raised out of the way as the key turns, by half of the bit, just as the other half strikes one ear of the slot in the bolt, and it drops into place again as soon as the bolt is thrown. A tapered iron spring riveted to the lock case keeps the tumber in tension, and should be strong enough to function even if, as sometimes happens, the lock must be mounted upside down to accommodate the hand of the door.

The cam that activates the latch bolt, and through which the knob shaft passes, is forged with a round stud riveted through a round hole in the face. The hole is tapered to allow filing smooth with the face and yet allow free movement of the cam. A scissors spring returns the latch bolt to locked position at each operation. Tension springs bear on the face side of the night bolt and the lock side of the dead bolt, to prevent chatter and unwanted movement should the door slam in the wind.

The case is made of three pieces: the face and ends in one sheet, bent at right angles; and top and bottom of tapered flat stock with studs riveted to them and the face plate. The backplate carries the one continuous ward of thin steel sheet, attached with tenons through the plate, and a tension spring to bear on the dead bolt. The continuous ward affords a complete track for the key through its travel, giving support against the pressure of the tumbler, and preventing wear at the keyhole, which would eventually cause the key to wobble and damage other parts.

The keeper for this type of lock is made in similar fashion to the case, with back end of tapered forged stock, and stud construction. Fine locks were fitted with a quarter-round brass striking strip at the lock edge, for the beveled end of the latch bolt, and to match the brass knobs. Cases usually were painted black inside and out, with all moving parts drawfiled bright to avoid friction. In all locks, oil is an enemy, for it attracts dust, which builds up and causes wear. Graphite is a better lubricant.

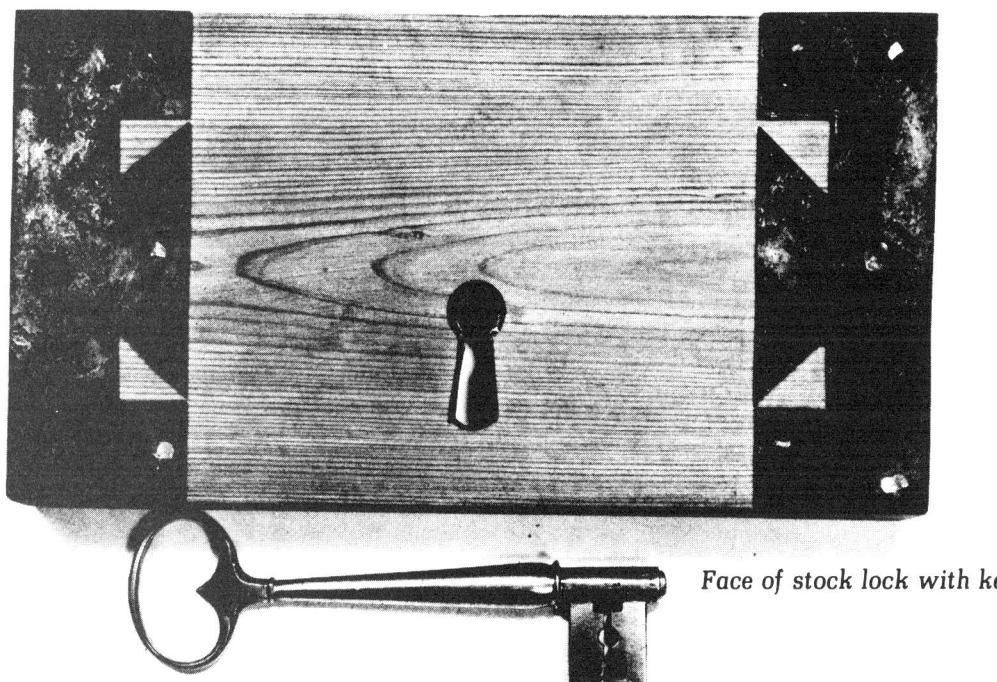

Face of stock lock with key.

Stock lock works on plate.

STOCK LOCK

Stock is a word that traditional English lock trades gave to locks with wooden cases, similar to the use of the term *stock* to indicate the wooden part of a gun. Thus, a stock lock is one with a wooden case. These were cheaper to make than iron ones, but they also had special uses. Since they had fewer iron parts, they were less subject to rust, and were chosen for use in places where dampness might impair iron locks, as on cellar and church doors or gates.

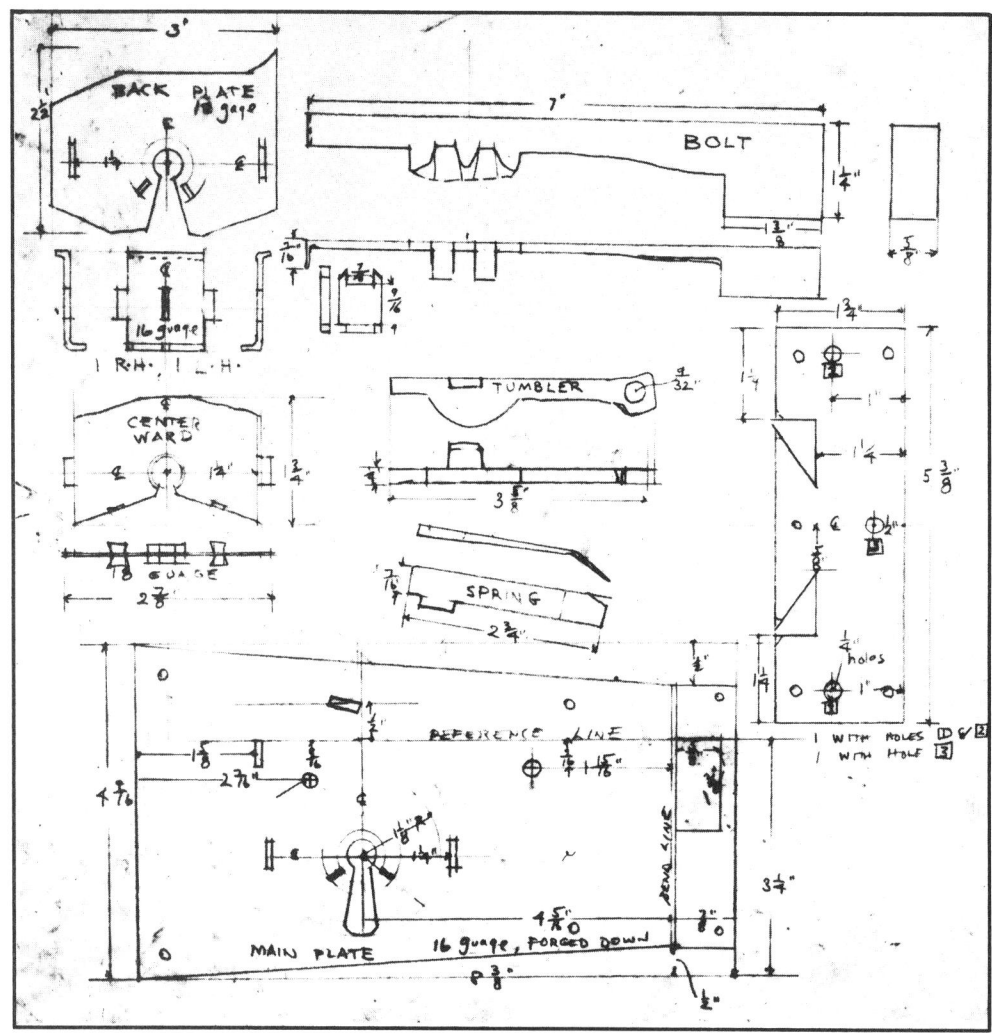

Shop drawing for stock lock.

Trimming an escutcheon in the vise.

They were of two types. Plain stock locks, called Banbury locks, had all parts embedded in the wood and were the cheapest form. Plate stock locks were made with all parts mounted on an iron plate, and the lock set into the wood case as a unit. Usually they were simple dead-bolt locks, with no auxiliary bolts, but mechanically they were the same as iron dead-bolt locks of similar form.

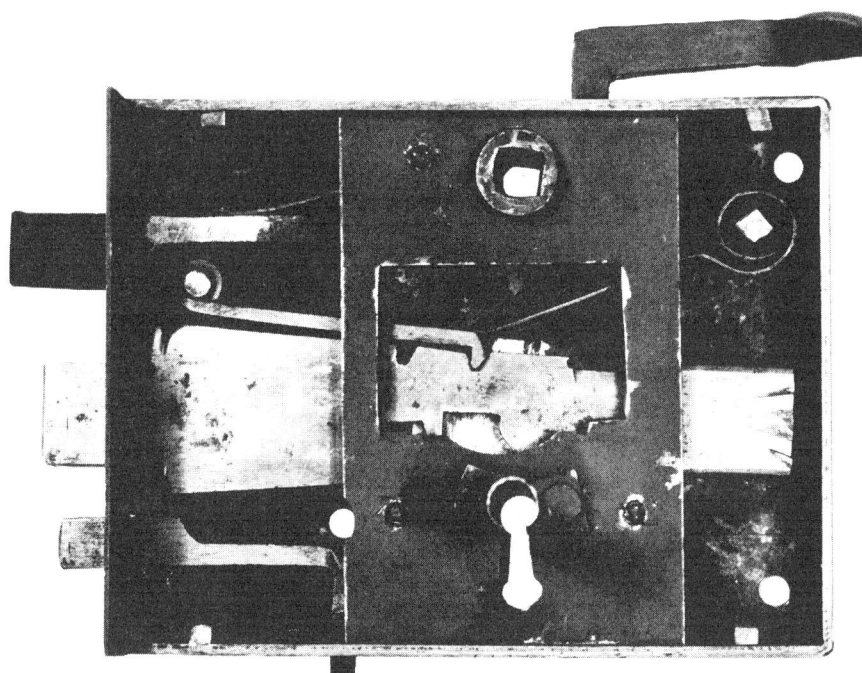

GERMAN IRON RIM LOCK

German-type rim lock, interior, backplate pierced to show bolt and tumbler action.

German locks differ in design from the English, and present other forging choices. Lever handles replace brass knobs, and the latch bolt moves vertically rather than horizontally. Keys often are made with asymmetrical bits, so no shoulders are necessary to stop the key in its right place. Since the keyhole matches the profile of the key bit, the key cannot pass entirely through the lock, but butts up against the opposite side of the case in operating position. Thus, keys can be forged in one piece, so no hindrance to filing exists in the form of a shoulder. Shafts are supported by passing through a tube or sleeve riveted to the backplate and extending through the door and escutcheon, assuring constant fit.

Again, all dimensions are taken from the key, with room for all parts to move, but with no wasted space. Unlike the English locks, which

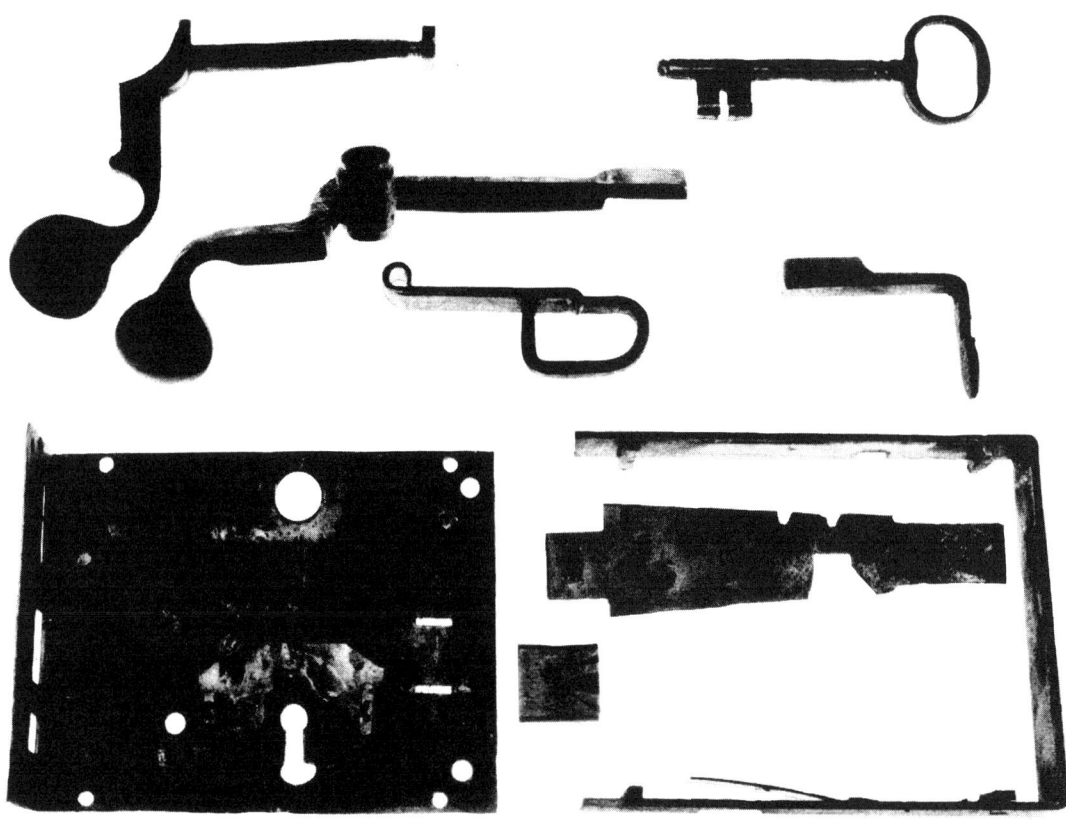

Case and main lock parts.

were bolted together for easy removal for repair, key fitting, or replacement, German ones usually were riveted together, thereby assuring that the lockmaker would be called to make any changes.

Although cases are studded, here the rim is one strip, running around the lock sides from front top to bottom, with no tapered bars for sides.

To forge the main lever handle and latch bar, use square stock of suitable size for the lock, here one-half inch, and forge it to shape, bending two square-cornered right angles in the flat section, and leaving a lump at the end for the press. Form a square collar long enough to go clear through the lock, with a tapered square hole to receive the shaft of the other handle, using a preforged taper mandrel to size the hole. Finish forging the press in a hollow anvil die, and file to shape.

When the taper mandrel can enter the collar horizontally and squarely, file the collar to fit snugly in the inside corner of the latch bar, flux both parts, and clamp together. The joint can be

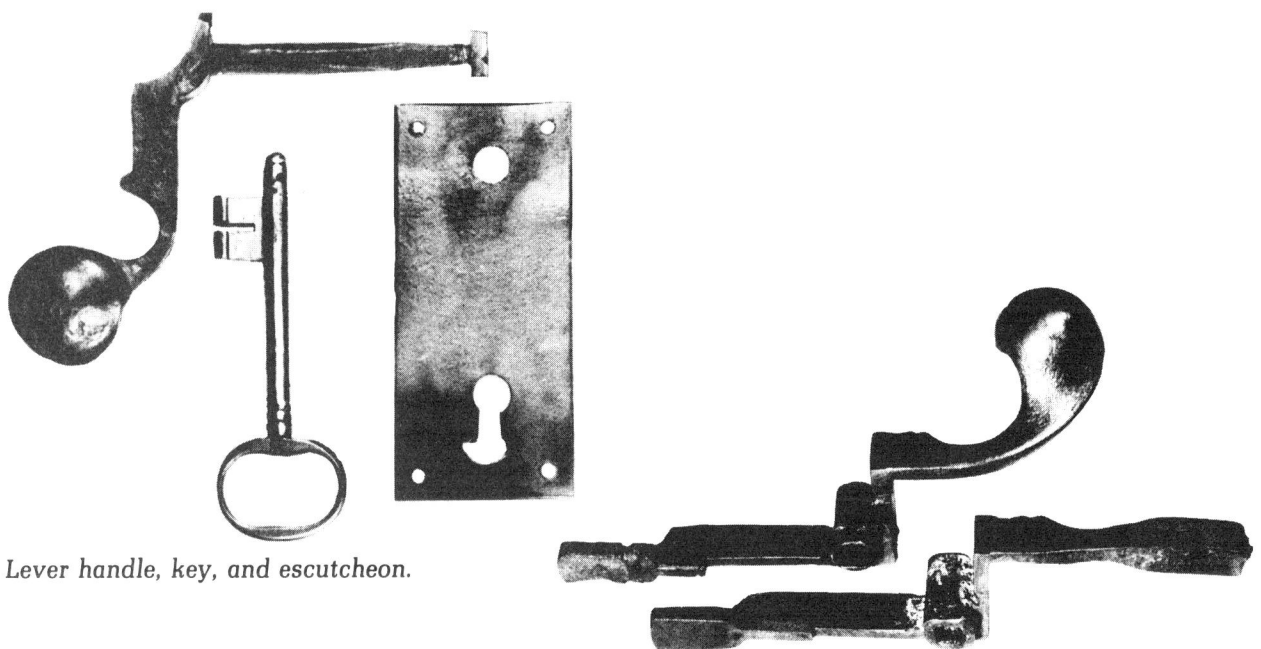

Lever handle, key, and escutcheon.

An original handle, and rough forging for a copy.

brazed in the forge, using brass spelter, or with a torch using a brazing rod. Either way, make sure that the brass runs throughout the joint. Brass is the traditional metal for brazing, since it melts at a lower heat than copper, and is strong enough for the purpose. After the joint is made, file both ends of the collar round to form studs that will rotate in holes in the case.

Two flat coil springs are required for latch bar and tumbler. Make these of spring steel, or mild steel cold-hammered enough to work harden to stiffness. If mild steel is used, do not heat for tempering, for this will remove all springiness. Start the spring around square studs, to be riveted to the case, making five bends around the stud, to keep the square tight, and then complete the coil. In order to provide space between the coils to allow movement of the spring, some separation is needed during the forming. The traditional German technique was to grease the surface of the strip and sprinkle sand upon it before bending, and wash it out afterward. However, this is sometimes difficult to remove, and sometimes uneven. A strip of stiff paper will serve equally well, since the coil will be bent cold, resulting in some spring-

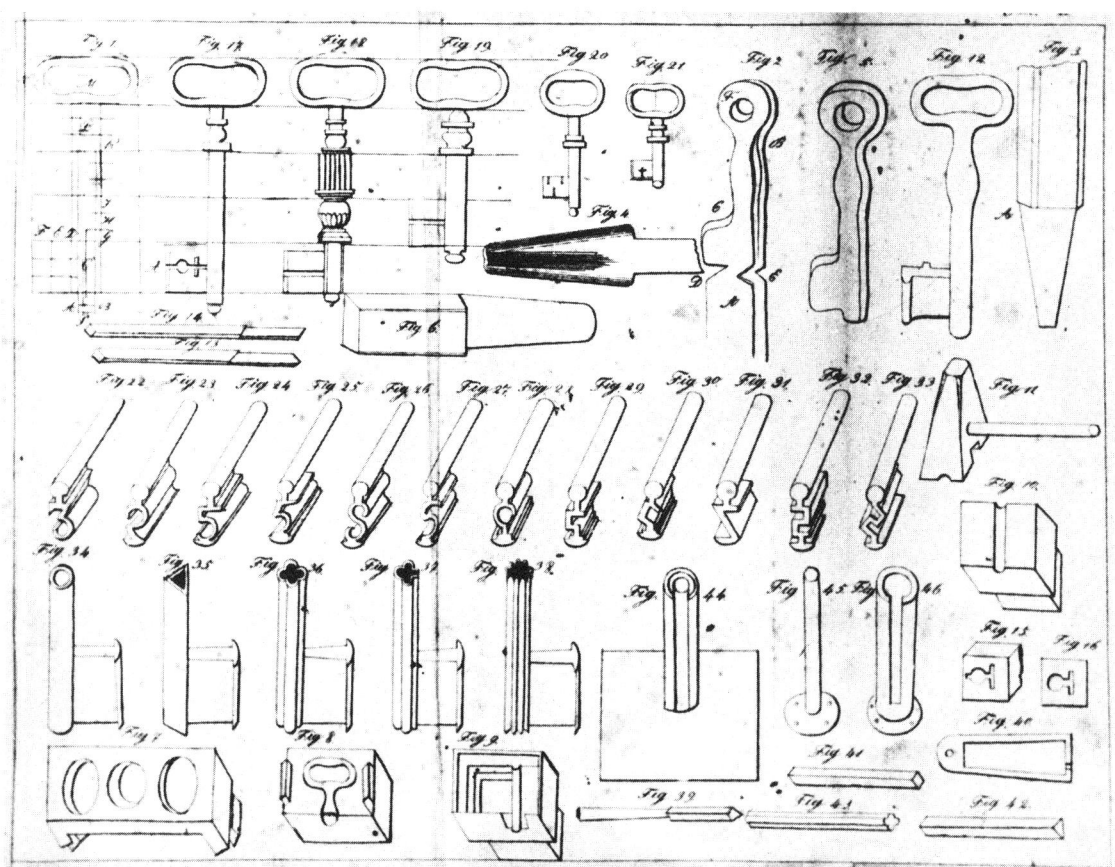

Plate from The Industrial Germany: Locksmithing, *Adam and Ferdinand Nagele, 1836, showing key and lock proportions and special tools. (Courtesy of William Ball, Sr.)*

Die for forming seat and offset in lever handle.

back. The paper can be slid out, or will burn out in the tempering.

To temper, heat to a red and quench in oil. Burning off the oil a couple of times will produce the right temper.

Forge the other lever handle from a single bar of the same size as the first. To make the bearing for the escutcheon and the shaft, which will extend through the door and lock, a special tool is needed. The tool is similar in principle to a nail header. Forge and bend a blank to form the shaft, set it in the vise-held tool, and forge the hot iron down with a fuller, seating the bearing and at the same time making the curved offset. The tool is illustrated in use making a handle for a lever latch of somewhat different design, which is detailed in the shop drawing for that latch, on page 127.

After finishing the handle part, draw the shaft to size to fit the door thickness, thread its end, and make a nut for it.

GERMAN
LEVER LATCH

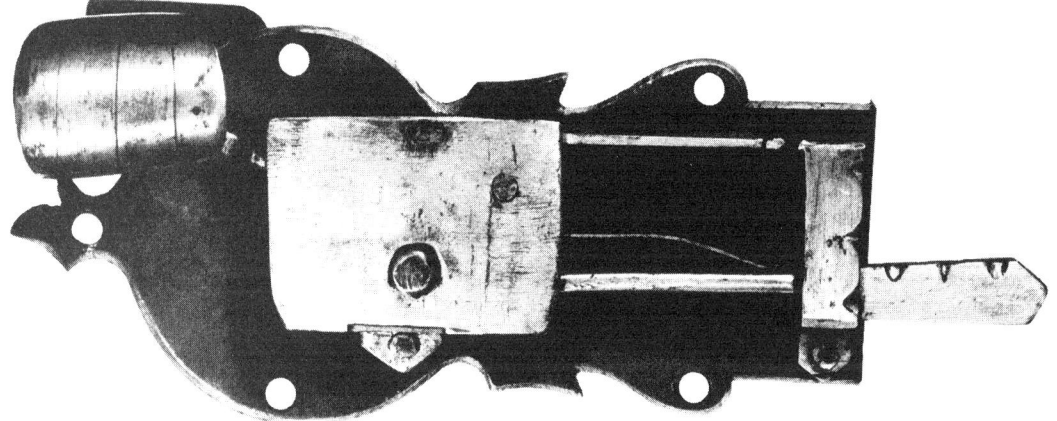

German-type lever latch.

Forging for this latch is much the same as for the German lock, its main elements being the lever handles. However, this type illustrates another method of making the handles. Instead of brazing a collar to the latch bar for the opposite handle shaft, use a threaded stud and screw the handle in place.

Forge the latch bar handle as before, but instead of the collar, punch a square hole in a block left in the corner, and fit the stud into it. After trying the square stud for fit, forge or file a round section for the thread, and wind a narrow strip of paper around it in a spiral, leaving a narrow space between the coils. Along this spiral space file a groove with a rat-tail file, making a male thread on the stud. Wrap a piece of wire in the groove, and unscrew. This makes the female thread.

Forge the other handle in the same way as the first. No shaft is needed in this case, just a round short stud the diameter of the outside of the coiled wire. Form and weld a round pipe sleeve, the same size inside, and long enough to go most of the way through the door. Braze the wire inside the tube, leaving enough room at one end for the stud on the handle.

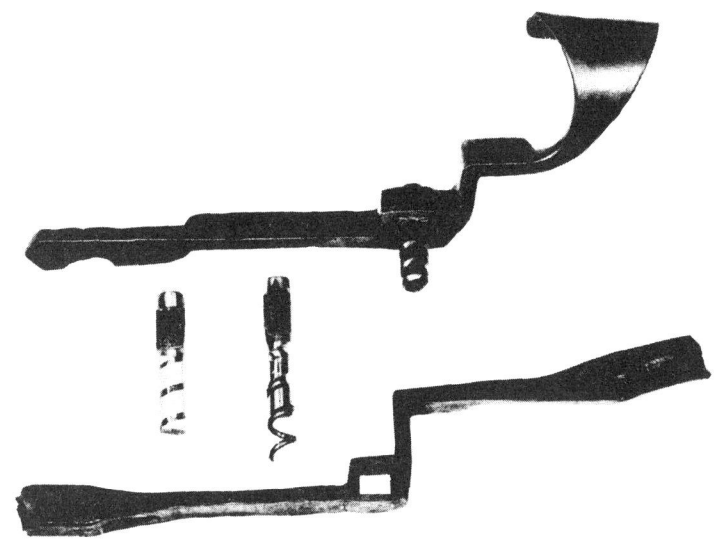

An original handle (top), with forged copy, stud, and screw.

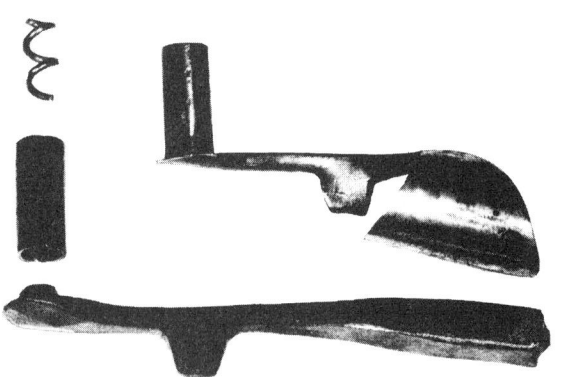

Expanded view of screw, collar, handle, and assembled parts.

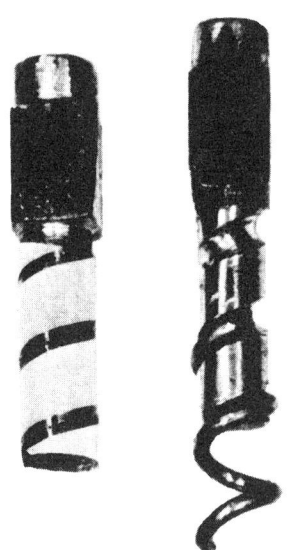

Detail of screw stud.

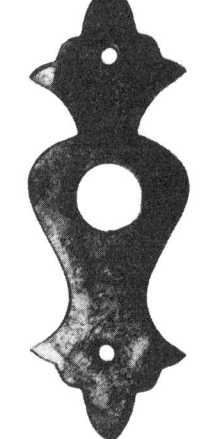

Escutcheon for the latch.

Finish forge the handle, file to shape, and braze to the threaded sleeve in such a position that when it is screwed up tight, the handle will lie horizontal. This requires a little rehearsal before brazing all together. In the absence of suitable taps and dies, early smiths often employed this method in making screws for their vises.

A decorative escutcheon, cut and bevel filed, completes the latch, with a rat-tail keeper for the catch.

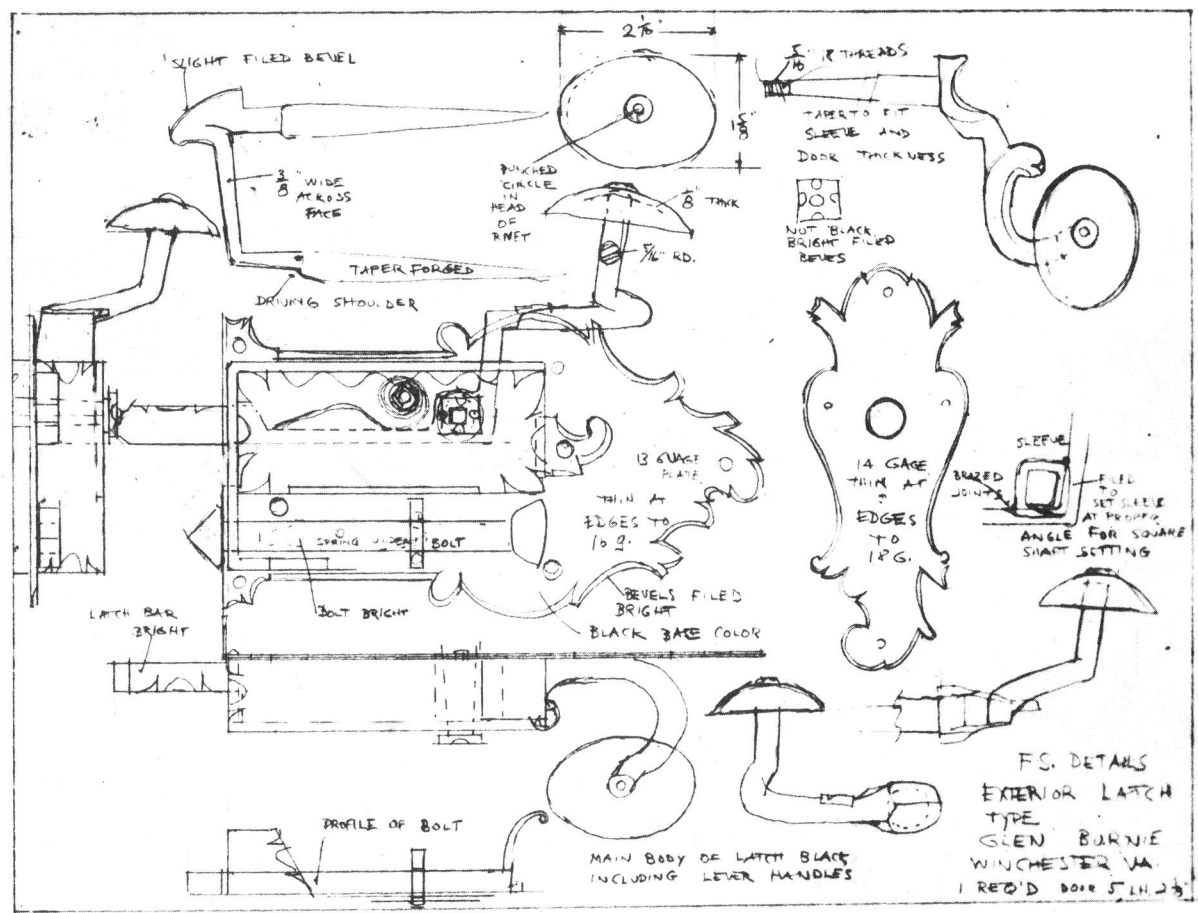

Shop drawing for a German-type lever latch.

PADLOCK

German padlock makers, and doubtless others, sometimes used this form of thread in making the key, which was a tube-and-ring bow with a bearing collar. The bolt was kept in the locked position by a coil spring. To open the lock the key is screwed up tight, pulling back the bolt and releasing the yoke.

Padlock, whose key is a wire-threaded sleeve.

GLOSSARY

anneal. Controlled cooling of hot steel, to avoid strains from the forging.

anvil. See illustration, page 4.

arbor press. Hand press for broaching holes, light bending, straightening.

beak. Small anvil tool with a rounded horn, or beak.

bevel file. To file edges at an angle to the surface.

Beverly shear. Trade name of a particular shear.

bickern. See illustration, page 8.

boss. A section of iron rising above the forged surface.

brazed. Iron parts joined with melted brass.

chamfer. To forge or file corners on flat or square iron.

chase, verb. To produce incised designs in iron or other metals with steel chisels or punches.

clefts. Slots in key bits to pass wards in the lock.

descale. To remove the oxide (scale) from forged work.

draw. To stretch iron by hammering.

drawfile. To file a smooth flat surface by drawing the file transversely along the work.

drift. Punch or punches used to refine or alter the shape of holes drilled or punched in iron.

faggot weld. End of a bar folded back on itself several times and welded together to increase size.

flash. Surplus metal squeezed out when forging in spring dies.

flux, noun. Material, often borax, used in welding, which, by melting and flowing, seals the joint surfaces against oxidation.

flux, verb. To apply flux during welding operations.

forge/finish forge. To work iron with the hammer.

fuller. A round-nosed tool used to stretch iron by striking it with a hammer. See illustration, page 12.

harden. To quench hot tool steel in liquid.

hardy. Anvil tool for cutting iron. See illustration, page 12.

hinge-eye bender. Tool for forming hinge eyes.

hot-cutter. Chisel for cutting hot iron.

hot shut, noun. A crack in iron caused by the metal being folded over itself and then forged.

jig. Any device to hold work in position for forging or other work.

lap weld. Weld where ends of bars are joined by lapping.

leg vise. Traditional blacksmiths' vise of ancient form.

mandrel. An iron or steel form for shaping rings.

neck bolt. A bolt with an offset shaft.

nibbler. A machine for cutting sheet-steel forms by rapid punching.

notcher. A punch for notching corners in sheet iron.

passivate. To neutralize the corroding effect of acid.

pintle. The hook on which a strap hinge swings.

planish, verb. To smooth and harden a surface with a hammer.

reveal, noun. Distance between a wall and the window casing.

scarf. To prepare a joint for welding by forging.

scriber. A scratch awl for marking lines in metal.

set hammer. A hammer to be set in position by the smith and struck by the helper.

shut, noun. See hot shut.

spelter. Granulated brass used in brazing.

swage. Anvil tool for forming iron shapes.

temper. The degree of hardness in a tool.

template. Form or pattern for forging or cutting.

thumb-latch cusp. Part of the thumb-latch grasp fastened to the door.

T weld. Two bars welded together in a T shape.

tinning. Coating iron with melted tin.

upset, upsetting, verbs. To increase cross-section by forging. The opposite of drawing.

ward. Baffles placed in a lock to prevent use of the wrong key.

warding file. Thin files for filing clefts in keys.

work harden. To harden by hammering cold.

SOURCES OF SUPPLIES

Blacksmithing Organizations

Artist-Blacksmiths' Association of North America (ABANA)
PO Box 816
Farmington, Georgia 30638
Phone: (706) 310-1030
www.abana.org

> Thirty years ago, ABANA began with only twenty blacksmiths who had a vision. Their vision has unfolded with a membership that has grown to over 5,000 strong. The resurgence of the "lost" art of blacksmithing is unmistakably evident.

National Ornamental and Miscellaneous Metals Association (NOMMA)
1535 Pennsylvania Avenue
McDonough, Georgia 30253
Phone: (888) 516-8585
www.nomma.org

> Formed in 1958 to serve the ornamental and miscellaneous metals industry; members produce the full spectrum of ornamental and miscellaneous metalwork, ranging from railings to driveway gates, and from sculpture to light structural steel.

Manufacturers

Throatless Shears
Beverly Shear Manufacturing Corp.
3004 West 111th Street
Chicago, IL 60655
Phone: (773) 238-0003

Box and pad brake
Dreis and Krump Manufacturing Co.
481 Governors Highway, Suite 2
Peotone, IL 60468
Phone: (708) 258-1200
www.dreis-krump.com

Hand bench punch
Kidder Metalworking
805 Prim Road
Colchester, VT 05446
Phone: (877) 294-1400
www.kidder-mfg.com

Power Hammer
Little Giant Power Hammer
420 4th Corso
Nebraska City, NE 68410
Phone: (402) 873-6603
www.littlegianthammer.com

Rod cutters, bar, and plate shears
Marvel Manufacturing
3501 Marvel Drive
Oshkosh, WI 54902
Phone: (920) 236-7200
www.sawing.com

Suppliers-machinery and hand tools

Centaur Forge, Ltd.
117 North Spring Street
Burlington, Wisconsin 53105
Phone: (800) 666-9175
www.centaurforge.com

> General line of blacksmiths' and farriers' tools, supplies, and books.

G.E. Forge & Tool, Inc.
959 Highland Way
Grover Beach California 93433
Phone: (877) 433-6743

> Manufactures farrier hand tools and KB horseshoes

McMaster-Carr Supply Co.
PO Box 4355
Chicago, Illinois 60680
Locations also in Atlanta, Georgia; Cleveland, Ohio; Los Angeles, California; and Princeton, New Jersey
Phone: (630) 833-0300
www.mcmaster.com

> Offers most of the equipment listed in the manufacturers' list above, plus anvils, aprons, arbor presses, brakes, forges, hand and bench punches and shears, sheet metal machines and tools, and more.

Pieh Tool Company, Inc.
661 Howards Road, Suite J
Camp Verde, Arizona 86322
Phone: (928) 554-0700
www.piehtoolco.com

> General line of blacksmiths' and farriers' tools, supplies, and books.

Index

Building the shop in Iona, NJ, about 1938.

The finished shop with Donald Streeter's handmade sign.

Hardware for sale in the show-room of the shop. Photos on the wall show buildings that were restored using Donald Streeter hardware.

Donald Streeter in the early days at the forge in his shop in Iona, NJ, 1940s.

Still hard at work in the 1960s. He took this of himself using an old box camera he used to photograph hardware for his catalog.